INDIANS

M E M O R I E S

The Most Memorable
Heroes, Heartaches & Highlights
from the Past 50 Seasons of Cleveland Indians Baseball

TIM LONG & DON FOX

GRAY & COMPANY, PUBLISHERS · CLEVELAND

Dedicated to Herb Score ...

Who better represents Indians memories than Cleveland's voice of summer? Whether we're catching a Tribe game while driving the car on a weekend errand, listening late at night to a Tribe West Coast game, or following the radio play-by-play while actually at the Stadium or Jacobs Field, for thirty-four years Herb has been our vocal link to Indians baseball. Through the good times and the (mostly) bad, thanks for the memories, Herb.

Copyright © 1997 by Tim Long and Don Fox

Cover photo courtesy of the Cleveland Press Collection, Cleveland State University Archives.

Gray & Company, Publishers
1588 E. 40th Street
Cleveland, Ohio 44103-2302
www.grayco.com

ISBN 1-886228-16-7   LC 97-45292
Printed in the United States of America
10 9 8 7 6 5 4 3 2 1

Introduction

A baseball team's tradition is built upon the loyalty and memories of its fans. Nowhere is this more evident than in Cleveland, where Tribe fans have witnessed the best and the worst. Through the golden era of Indians baseball from 1948 to 1954, the dark ages of the 1960s, '70s, and '80s (when threats to move the Indians were as common as lake effect snow in winter), to the renaissance of the 1990s, Indians fans have experienced it all: the joys of a world championship, the burden of seemingly endless losing seasons, and then resurrected hopes of championship, with new heroes leading the charge in a beautiful new ballpark. Whatever era holds your most cherished Indians memories, we are are all bound together by the distinctive ability to make it through the tough times while savoring the recollections of the good. To be sure, Tribe fans share a rich tradition that sustains itself with many memorable players, games, and exceptional events and personalities. This tradition keep us watching, listening to, and celebrating the game of baseball while we root-root-root for our home team. Go Tribe!

Acknowledgments

We would like to thank the Cleveland Indians organization for their assistance in setting up interviews with former players and broadcast personnel. Of special note is the help received from Bob DiBiasio, Vice President of Indians Public Relations, and public relations specialist Curtis Danberg.

Grateful acknowledgment is made to *The Plain Dealer* for permission to reproduce the content of various headlines and articles. These items are reprinted with all rights reserved to *The Plain Dealer*. We also offer special thanks to *The Plain Dealer* for the use of Dick Dugan's caricatures.

Special thanks to the Cleveland Press Collection at the Cleveland State University Archives for permission to reproduce various articles and pictures, and for the help of CSU archivist Bill Becker for his generous research assistance.

Thanks to the wonderful staffs at the following public libraries: the Cleveland Public Library, the Rocky River Public Library, and the Mayfield Branch of the Cuyahoga County Public Library.

And thanks to everyone who shared their Indians memories.

INDIANS

MEMORIES

1 **The Indians flag flying atop the Terminal Tower,** telling fans "there's a game today."

2 **Indians Record.** The longest measured home run in Cleveland Municipal Stadium was hit by Indians first baseman Luke Easter on June 23, 1950, a drive Easter hit 477 feet from home plate into Section 4 of the upper deck.

3 **Larry Doby.** The Indians' great center fielder was the first African-American player to enter the American League when he signed a contract on July 3, 1947, to play for the Tribe. He played 10 of his 13 major-league seasons with Cleveland, finishing his career with a lifetime .283 batting average, 253 home runs, and 969 RBIs.

4 **Nicknames:** Rocky "The Rock" Colavito, OF, 1955–1959, 1965–1967. Perhaps the most popular player to ever don a Cleveland uniform. When he was in a slump, the popular saying around Cleveland was "Don't knock the Rock."

5   **Memorable Game:** Game 6 of the 1995 American League Championship Series vs. Seattle in the Kingdome. Seemingly all of Cleveland was glued to the television the night of October 17, 1995 as the Tribe won its first American League pennant in 41 years, shutting out the Mariners 4–0. Who can forget Kenny Lofton scoring all the way from second base on a passed ball in the eighth inning?

INDIANS 4 *Playoffs '95* MARINERS 0

On to Atlanta!

6   **Indians Movies:** In 1949, Twentieth-Century Fox released the movie *The Kid from Cleveland*, about a troubled youth who befriends the 1948 Cleveland Indians baseball team. Player-manager Lou Boudreau remarked, "I would like to buy every print of the film and burn it. Boy, that picture was a dog."

7 **Duane Kuiper's home run.** The Tribe's second baseman from 1974 to 1981, Duane hit what turned out to be the only home run of his major league career on August 29, 1977. He later told reporters, "One home run is better than none, but any more than one and people start expecting them."

8 **Bill Veeck**, owner of the Indians from 1946 to 1949 and one of the most colorful personalities in Cleveland baseball history. Refusing to wear a tie, insisting he be called "Bill," igniting fireworks at games, promoting "Ladies Day" games, and hiring circus performers to appear in games, Veeck brought a unique enthusiasm for the game and the fans. His promotions combined with an exceptional Indians team to break five different major league attendance records in the world series championship season of 1948: single-game attendance, doubleheader attendance, night game attendance, opening day attendance, and total season attendance (2,620,627).

9   **Good Trade:** On November 29, 1971, the Indians acquired pitcher Gaylord Perry and shortstop Frank Duffy from the San Francisco Giants for pitcher Sam McDowell. McDowell had been a strikeout leader with the Tribe since 1961 and was balanced on the edge of greatness. Perry won 24 games for the Tribe in 1972 and captured the Cy Young award and went on to win 19 games in 1973 and 21 in 1974. McDowell won only 19 games total after he left Cleveland.

10   **John Adams and his drum.** Adams has beat his drum through bad and good in the bleachers at Municipal Stadium and Jacobs Field since 1973. He has season tickets for himself, his wife, and his drum.

11   **Reaching the top of the ramp at Cleveland Municipal Stadium** and seeing the vast expanse of the emerald-green grass of the outfield, then hearing the sound of the crack of the bat as players took batting practice before the game.

Recollections . . .

Nev Chandler, Cleveland sportscaster, on his disappointment of not seeing Rocky Colavito in a familiar Indians uniform:

"I went to the opener [Opening Day, 1960] and sat in the upper deck behind home plate. I saw Rocky in a Tigers uniform and I couldn't believe it. I actually cried. I was fourteen years old."

12 **Retired Uniform Numbers:** Few accomplishments in professional sports are as meaningful to players as having one's uniform number retired. The Indians have retired the following:

#3 Earl Averill, OF, 1929–1939; retired in 1965.
#5 Lou Boudreau, SS, 1938–1950; retired in 1970.
#14 Larry Doby, OF, 1947–1955, 1958; retired in 1994.
#18 Mel Harder, P, 1928–1947; retired in 1990.
#19 Bob Feller, P, 1936–1956; retired in 1957.

13 **Why hasn't Bob Lemon's No. 21 been retired by the team?** Lemon, who played his entire career with the Indians (1941–1942, 1946–1958) and won 20 or more games in a single season seven different times, was inducted into the Baseball Hall of Fame in 1976.

14 **Herb Score-isms:** Former Indians pitcher Herb Score entered the broadcast booth in 1963 after his playing career ended. Herb's descriptions of games on television and radio informed fans for over 30 years, often in quite interesting ways. One favorite Score-ism: "Swing and a miss, that's a called strike three!"

15 **Leroy "Satchel" Paige**, Tribe pitcher from 1948 to 1949, was rumored to be nearly 50 years old when he joined the team. "Satch" never revealed his age, but instead asked the age-old question, "How old would you have to be if you didn't know how old you were?"

16 **The playoff game of 1948.** The Indians and Boston Red Sox made history on October 4, 1948, when they played in the first-ever single play-off game to decide the American League championship. The Indians had a two-game lead with three games remaining in the 1948 season. They lost two of three to Detroit, and Boston beat the Yankees two of three to force a tie. The Tribe traveled to Boston and beat the Red Sox 8–3 for the right to face Boston's National League team, the Braves, in the World Series. 1948 was truly a "one-game season."

PITTSBURGH POST-GAZETTE
80TH YEAR—NO. 229

CLEVELAND PLAIN DEALER

CLEVELAND, TUESDAY MORNING, OCTOBER 5, 1948   16 PAGES   FIVE CENTS   FINAL

INDIANS WIN FIRST PENNANT IN 28 YEARS; BEARDEN VICTOR, 8-3

17 **Rookie of the Year:** In 1955, hard-throwing lefthander Herb Score was named AL Rookie of the Year by the Baseball Writers of America. He finished with 16 wins and 10 losses and struck out 245 batters in 227 innings pitched. Harry Jones of *The Plain Dealer* called him "the heir apparent to Feller's throne." The Indian's Hall of Fame outfielder Tris Speaker stated, "If nothing happens to him, this kid has got to be the greatest!"

18 **Indians Luck:** In the first inning of the Indians game with the New York Yankees on May 7, 1957, Herb Score was hit in the right eye by a line drive off the bat of Yankee Gil McDougald. The injury was serious enough to sideline Herb for the entire 1957 season. Some say it was this injury that destroyed his career; Herb, however, claims it was a torn tendon in his elbow suffered early in the 1958 season that hurt his career the most. Whatever the reason, baseball and the Tribe lost one of the most promising pitchers of all time.

SCORE HIT IN EYE BY LINE DRIVE

19 **Sports Illustrated Covers:** The cover of *SI*'s 1987 baseball season-preview issue featured Joe Carter and Cory Snyder as the fire behind an "Indian Uprising."

20 **The consistency of Tribe utility-player John Lowenstein.** Lowenstein batted exactly .242 in 1974, 1976, and 1977. To achieve this feat, he needed to go hitless in his last game of the 1977 season. As he struck out in his last at-bat, his teammates hugged him at home plate in celebration. After the game, Lowenstein said, "Team success takes priority. But there is something to be said for personal glory as well." In 1975, Lowenstein was plagued by injuries and batted only .205.

21 **Nicknames:** "Sudden" Sam McDowell, P, 1961–1971. The sheer speed of this hard-throwing lefthander's fastballs prompted scouts and players alike to claim that his pitches were "suddenly" upon you, before you even knew it. Umpire Bill Kinnon remarked, "he was so quick there were times you weren't quite ready to call the pitch."

22 **Indians Hall of Famers:** The following pre-1948 players are legendary in Indians history, and were honored for their baseball feats by being inducted into the National Baseball Hall of Fame in Cooperstown:

Name	Pos.	Years	Inducted
Napoleon Lajoie	2B	1905–1914	1937
Tristam "Tris" Speaker	OF	1916–1926	1937
Elmer Flick	OF	1902–1910	1963
Stan Coveleski	P	1916–1924	1969
Earl Averill	OF	1929–1939	1975
Joe Sewell	SS	1920–1930	1977
Adrian "Addie" Joss	P	1902–1910	1978

Recollections . . .

Larry Doby remembers the classic photo showing him and Indians pitcher Steve Gromek hugging after winning Game 4 of the 1948 World Series, 2–1, against the Boston Braves on October 9, 1948:

"I will always cherish it because it showed that emotions can be put into a form that's something other than skin color...It was a wonderful moment."

23 **Frank Lane.** The mere mention of his name makes Tribe fans shudder and recoil in dismay. "Trader Lane" made 51 trades involving 118 players in his tenure as the club's general manager from 1957 to 1960. He will forever be remembered as the man who traded away fan favorite Rocky Colavito and slugger Roger Maris.

24 **Memorable Game:** Throughout the 1995 season, late inning heroics were normal for the Tribe. On June 4, the Indians trailed the Toronto Blue Jays 7–0 after one inning and faced pitcher David Cone, a Cy Young Award winner. The Tribe caught up to the Blue Jays by nibbling away at the Jays' lead until it was 8–6 Jays in the bottom of the ninth. With two outs, the Tribe scored a run and had a runner on first. The next batter, first baseman Paul Sorrento, hit the first pitch into the right-field seats to win the game 9–8 in the most dramatic come-from-behind victory of 1995.

Jacobs Field magic

25 **Herb Score's radio broadcast partners:** Bob Neal, 1968–1972; Joe Tait, 1973–1979; Nev Chandler, 1980–1984; Steve Lamar, 1985–1987; Paul Olden, 1988–1989; and Tom Hamilton, 1990–1997.

26 **Real Names:** Indians pitcher Cal McLish hurled quite effectively for the Tribe from 1956 to 1959. His full name was Calvin Coolidge Julius Caesar Tuskahoma McLish. Cal was part American Indian, which at least explains "Tuskahoma."

27 **Bad Trade:** On December 15, 1959, Cal McClish was traded to the Cincinnati Reds along with first baseman Gordy Coleman and second baseman Billy Martin for Reds second baseman Johnny Temple. Coleman became the Reds starting first baseman and hit 54 homers during the 1961 and 1962 seasons, but McLish never made it with the Reds. Temple was traded away after the 1961 season.

28 **Citizens Night at the Stadium.** With the future of Cleveland baseball in doubt once more, Mayor George Voinovich initiated a campaign to prove to Major League Baseball executives that Clevelanders did indeed support the Tribe. At the mayor's urging, 61,340 fans showed up to see the Tribe beat Toronto 2–1 on "Citizens Night," May 23, 1986.

61,340 show Tribal loyalties

Indians thank citizens by whipping Jays, 3-1

29 **Sports Illustrated Covers:** Manny Ramirez represented the Indians on *SI's* cover as they got "Ready to Rock" on April 1, 1996.

30 **Indians Luck:** As the newly designated team captain, first baseman Vic Wertz broke his right ankle in a spring training exhibition game on March 30, 1958. Vic played in only 25 games during the 1958 season. Previously, in 1955, Vic missed the entire season as he recovered from a nonparalytic type of polio.

31 **The huge Chief Wahoo sign** above Gate A at Cleveland Municipal Stadium that announced game times and ticket availability for upcoming home stands. After the 1948 World Series victory, a special crown was hoisted over the Chief's head to signify the Tribe as world champs.

32 **Hitting for the Cycle:** Six tribesman have managed to hit a single, double, triple, and home run, all in a single game. The most recent was first baseman Andre Thornton, who singled in the first inning, tripled in the second, homered in the seventh, and doubled in the ninth against Boston in Fenway Park on April 22, 1978.

33   **World Champions.** The 1948 Indians won the World Series, four games to two, over the Boston Braves. When the team returned to Cleveland, 200,000 fans lined Euclid Avenue from Public Square to University Circle for a celebratory parade. Here are the champs of '48:

Indians roster for the World Series:

Manager: Lou Boudreau
Coaches: Mel Harder, William McKechnie, Harold Ruel

#2 John Berardino, IF
#3 Eddie Robinson, 1B
#4 Joe Gordon, 2B
#5 Lou Boudreau, SS
#6 Ken Keltner, 3B
#7 Al Rosen, 3B
#10 Jim Hegan, C
#12 Joe Tipton, C
#14 Larry Doby, CF
#16 Ed Klieman, P
#18 Russ Christopher, P
#19 Bob Feller, P

#20 Sam Zoldak, P
#21 Bob Lemon, P
#23 Don Black, P
#24 Bob Kennedy, OF*
#25 Bob Muncrief, P
#27 Steve Gromek, P
#28 Ray Boone, IF
#29 Satchel Paige, P
#30 Gene Bearden, P
#31 Allie Clark, OF
#32 Hank Edwards, RF
#34 Dale Mitchell, LF
#35 Walt Judnick, OF
#36 Hal Peck, OF
#38 Thurman Tucker, OF

Recollections . . .

Texas Rangers outfielder Jeff Burroughs, on seeing rowdy Cleveland fans jumping from the stands and running toward him on June 4, 1974, at the infamous "Ten Cent Beer Night" game:

"I felt like Custer at Little Big Horn."

No. 35227—Phone Cherry 1111   CLEVELAND, TUESDAY, OCTOBER 21, 1948

The Cleveland Press

The Newspaper That Serves Its Readers

***   34 Pages—3 Cents   HOME EDITION

200,000 CHEER OUR CHAMPIONS

34   **Memorable Game:** Game 4 of the 1997 World Series, at Jacobs Field in Cleveland, October 22, 1997. Tribe bats get hot despite the frigid conditions—38 degrees at game time, with a wind-chill factor of 18 degrees—the coldest World Series game since officials began recording game temperatures in 1975. With rookie playoff sensation Jaret Wright on the mound, the Indians forsake the brisk wind and occasional snowflakes to beat the Florida Marlins 10–3, evening the series at two games apiece.

35

Indians Managers: From 1948 to 1997, the Tribe has had 24 field bosses, averaging a new manager approximately every 32 months or so—not what you'd call job security!

Years	Manager	Record	Years	Manager	Record
1942–1950	Lou Boudreau	728–649	1968–1971	Alvin Dark	266–321
1951–1956	Al Lopez	570–354	1971	Johnny Lipon	18–41
1957–	Kerby Farrell	76–77	1972–1974	Ken Aspromonte	220–260
1958	Bobby Bragan	31–36	1975–1977	Frank Robinson	186–189
1958–1960	Joe Gordon	184–151	1977–1979	Jeff Torborg	157–201
1960	Jo Jo White	1–0	1979–1982	Dave Garcia	247–244
1960–1961	Jimmy Dykes	104–114	1983	Mike Ferraro	40–60
1961	Mel Harder	0–1	1983–1987	Pat Corrales	280–355
1962	Mel McGaha	80–82	1987–1989	Doc Edwards	173–207
1963–1966	Birdie Tebbetts	311–298	1989	John Hart	8–11
1966	George Strickland	15–24	1990–1991	John McNamara	102–137
1967	Joe Adcock	75–87	1991–	Mike Hargrove	535–453

36 **Sports Illustrated Covers:** The Tribe first graced the cover of *Sports Illustrated* on April 18, 1955. Legendary third baseman Al Rosen was featured.

37 **Rookie of the Year:** The Tribe's young first baseman and slugger Chris Chambliss was voted the best rookie player in the American League in 1971. At 22, Chambliss batted .275, with nine home runs and 48 runs batted in. After two more solid seasons with the Tribe where he flirted with a .300 batting average, Chambliss was traded to the New York Yankees on April 27, 1974, along with pitchers Dick Tidrow and Cecil Upshaw, for Yankee pitchers Fritz Peterson, Steve Kline, Fred Beene, and Tom Buskey. Once again, the Indians were guilty of sacrificing quality for quantity.

38 **The So-Called "Curse."** After being fired by Tribe general manager Frank Lane in 1958, Manager Bobby Bragan reportedly placed a hex on the Indians fortunes forever. In his book *You Can't Hit the Ball with the Bat on Your Shoulder*, Bragan denied the story about the curse but remarked that "having Lane as the general manager was curse enough."

39 **Play-by-play announcer Jimmy Dudley,** with his unique voice and style, broadcast games from 1948 to 1967. Who can forget his call of a home run—"That ball's going, going . . . gone!"—or a double play—"Over to second, one away, back to first . . . it's a double play!" (And, of course, his aluminum siding commercial, "Garfield 1—2323.") He was inducted into the Baseball Hall of Fame's Media Wing in 1997.

40 **Nicknames:** Leon "Daddy Wags" Wagner, OF, 1964–1967. The regular left fielder during his time in Cleveland, Leon got his nickname from the slogan that promoted his Los Angeles clothing store: "Get Your Rags From Daddy Wags." After missing a fly ball during a night game at Cleveland Stadium, Wagner, in a memorable postgame interview, explained, "I lost it in the glare of the full moon."

41 **Bad Trade:** Another Frank Lane beauty. First baseman Norm Cash was traded to the Detroit Tigers for third baseman Don Demeter on April 12, 1960. Cash went on to play 17 years in the major leagues, winning the American League batting title in 1961 and hitting a career total 377 home runs. Demeter played in only 15 major league games.

42   **The smooth double-play combination** of shortstop Lou Boudreau and second baseman Joe Gordon from 1947 to 1950.

43   **Spring training sites.** Before settling Tucson in 1947, spring training was held in a number of locations. Notable stops along the way were Clearwater, Florida; Dallas, Texas; Macon, Georgia; and New Orleans, Louisiana.

44   **The Return of Early Wynn.** Having left the Indians after the 1957 season, the 43-year-old Wynn rejoined the Tribe with 299 career victories in June 1963. Wynn won the coveted 300th game of his career, a milestone for any pitcher, on July 13, 1963. He was the fourth pitcher to gain 300-victory status.

45   **Player-Manager:** Mike Hargrove began his playing career in 1974 and joined the Indians in 1979. As a first baseman, Mike was a steady performer for the Tribe until he was released in 1985. After managing in the minor leagues and serving as an Indians coach, he became the team's skipper on July 6, 1991, succeeding John McNamara.

Recollections . . .

Pete Franklin, former Sportsline radio host in Cleveland (1966–1988) and now a sports radio talk-show host at radio station KNBR in San Francisco, recalls the Indians–Yankees rivalry:

"I always hated the New York Yankees. When owner George Steinbrenner and manager Billy Martin led them in the 1970s, I was looking for some gimmick to hype the Cleveland fans into sharing my hatred of the Yankees. On my Sportsline radio show, I announced the creation of the 'I Hate the Yankees Hankie.' They were introduced for the fans to wave at a Indians-Yankees doubleheader at Municipal Stadium on September 5, 1977. Well, the Tribe swept the Yankees in that doubleheader and Billy Martin was incensed. The idea of the 'hankie' became popular around the American League after that, and I was proud to have been a part of being a 'pain in the you-know-what' for Martin and Steinbrenner."

46

Bad Trade, Bad Trade: Most Tribe fans will never forget the stunning trade of popular slugger Rocky Colavito to the Detroit Tigers for outfielder Harvey Kuenn on April 17, 1960. Colavito continued to have very productive years, while Kuenn's fortunes faded. What may not be remembered is who the Tribe gave away in 1965 to reacquire Colavito from the Chicago White Sox: young outfielder Tommy Agee and pitcher Tommy John. Agee went on to become the American League Rookie of the Year in 1966 and Tommy John, a valuable left-handed pitcher, went on to great success with the White Sox, Los Angeles Dodgers, and New York Yankees. A mitigating factor: Colavito's presence in Cleveland from 1965 to 1967 may have spurred enough fan interest to keep the Indians in Cleveland.

TRIBE GETS KUENN IN COLAVITO TRADE

47 **Indians Books:** *The Curse of Rocky Colavito*, by Terry Pluto (Simon and Schuster, 1994). As the subtitle of this book indicates, this is "a loving look at a thirty-year slump." A must for the long-suffering Tribe fan.

48 **Nicknames:** Mike "Big Bear" Garcia, P, 1948–1959. Mike possessed such a husky build that he resembled a real grizzly. "The Bear" finished his career with 142 wins, 96 losses, and 1,095 strikeouts, having pitched in 397 games for the Indians.

49 **Indians Luck:** The disastrous home plate collision of Cincinnati Reds third baseman Pete Rose and Indians catcher Ray Fosse in the 1970 All-Star Game. Rose plowed into Fosse at full speed as the Tribe's star catcher waited for the throw from the outfield. Fosse's young career was definitely affected—he suffered a severe shoulder injury from which he never fully recovered. Speaking about the collision afterwards, Ray said, "Well, that's football!"

50 **Family Affair:** The Perry brothers, Jim and Gaylord, both starred for the Tribe. Older brother Jim pitched for the Indians from 1959 to 1963 and again from 1974 to 1975. Gaylord steadied the pitching staff from 1972 to 1975.

51 **Tribe Trivia:** Slugger Rocky Colavito is known mostly for his bat. But in 1958 he took the mound as a relief pitcher and hurled three scoreless innings, walking three batters and striking out one against the Detroit Tigers, to whom Colavito was traded in 1960.

52 **Nicknames:** "The Human Rain Delay," Mike Hargrove, 1B, 1979–1985. Prior to becoming an Indians coach and manager, Hargrove as a player practiced a hat-straightening, cleat-knocking ritual before stepping into the batter's box. His machinations drove pitchers, umpires, and fans positively nuts and further slowed the pace of the leisurely grand old game.

53 **Perfection:** The 1965 season saw Rocky Colavito, in his second stint with the Tribe, perform flawlessly in the field as he played his right field position without an error.

54 **The Manager Trade.** In an unprecedented move, Indians general manager Frank "Trader" Lane sent his skipper, Joe Gordon, to the Detroit for Tiger manager Jimmy Dykes on August 3, 1960. Dykes remarked, "I bring no magic to the Indians, if I had any, I'd have used it on the Tigers." He was right. Dykes guided the Indians to a fourth-place finish in 1960 and was fired with one game remaining in 1961. It was the only time in major league history that two teams have traded managers.

55 **"Mobile seating" at cavernous Cleveland Municipal Stadium.** Fans attending home games could run from section to section, from lower to upper deck, and take in the game from a variety of vantage points. With crowds that sometimes numbering only in the hundreds, stadium ushers didn't force fans to move from choice seats for which they didn't have tickets. Ah, Indians baseball in the 1960s, 1970s, and 1980s!

56   **The Infamous Ten-Cent Beer Night.** At Cleveland Municipal Stadium on June 4, 1974, a thirsty crowd of 25,134 consumed mass quantities of beer. Some exuberant patrons took to the field as early as the sixth and seventh innings, but by the bottom of the ninth, with the Indians trailing 5–3, chaos reigned. Head umpire Nester Chylak called the game a forfeit to the Texas Rangers and deemed the Tribe fans "uncontrollable beasts." Game statistics: 60,000 cups of beer sold, nine fans arrested, seven treated at hospitals for minor injuries.

Stadium beer night fans riot, ending Indians' rally in forfeit

57   **20-Game Winner:** Gaylord Perry accomplished this feat twice while with the Tribe: 24–16 in 1972, and 21–13 in 1974.

58   **Good Trade:** On December 10, 1991, the Indians traded catcher Eddie Taubensee and pitcher Willie Blair to the Houston Astros for outfielder Kenny Lofton and second baseman Dave Rhode. This amounted to highway robbery, as Kenny Lofton developed into a premier outfielder and base stealer, helping lead the Tribe into the 1995 World Series.

59   **Indians Books:** *The Cleveland Indians Encyclopedia*, by Russell Schneider (Temple University Press, 1996). Russ Schneider's masterful work puts everything you'd ever want to know about the Tribe into this large volume. From stats, player profiles, and team history, the avid Tribe fan won't be left wanting. This book is spectacular.

60   **Indians Record:** Tribe hitters set a new team record when they clubbed eight home runs in one game, against the Milwaukee Brewers on April 25, 1997. Leading the way were third baseman Matt Williams with three; outfielder Dave Justice with two; and Manny Ramirez, Chad Curtis, and Sandy Alomar with one each.

61 **The Catch.** Willie Mays's miraculous over-the-head catch of a Vic Wertz would-be home run in the 1954 World Series planted that game in baseball history. In the seventh inning of Game 1 against the New York Giants, Indians first baseman Vic Wertz sent a smashing drive to center field of the Polo Grounds in New York, some 460 feet from home plate. Mays turned his back to home and hauled the ball in. Perhaps more remarkable was the throw into the infield that prevented Larry Doby from scoring from second base. Because of the configuration of the Polo Grounds, Wertz's blast would have been a home run in any other major league ballpark. The Indians went on to lose the series in four straight games.

62 **Indians infielder Johnny Berardino** (1948–1950, 1952) was perhaps better known as Dr. Steve Hardy on the daytime soap opera *General Hospital.* Team owner Bill Veeck reportedly insured Berardino's face during the 1949 season in the event that an injury would derail his promising acting career. As a child, Berardino played in the *Our Gang* serials of the 1930s.

Recollections . . .

Rocco Scotti, professional singer and longtime performer of the National Anthem at Cleveland Indians games from 1974 to 1993, recalls a trip to the Big Apple:

"Not only did I sing the National Anthem at Indians games, but George Steinbrenner often flew me into New York to kickoff the Yankees games. In a nationally televised game in New York, I started the National Anthem, when all of a sudden I felt a gnat or mosquito in my throat. I panicked and didn't think I'd be able to continue. Somehow I struggled through and when it was over, I began coughing and couldn't stop. The Yankees'Yogi Berra came rushing over and said,'Hey Rocco, what's the matter?'I told him a mosquito had gotten me in the larynx. Yogi looked at me and said,'Boy, it's a good thing it didn't get your voice box.'"

63 **Bad Trade:** At the outset of the 1974 season, the Indians were in need of a left-handed relief pitcher. On April 3, 1974, they traded one of their minor league prospects to the Los Angeles Dodgers for lefty Bruce Ellingsen. Who was the prospect traded for Ellingsen? None other than Pedro Guerrero, the third baseman-outfielder who had a spectacular National League career with the Dodgers and St. Louis Cardinals. Guerrero retired from baseball with a .300 lifetime average. Ellingsen's only season in the majors was 1974.

64 **Vic Power's fielding.** Although he may be better remembered for his daring attempts at stealing home, first baseman Power also won Gold Gloves for his defensive play in every year he played for the Indians—1958, 1959, 1960, and 1961.

65 **Tribe Trivia:** The baseball movie *The Natural* (1984), starring Robert Redford as Roy Hobbs, featured an appearance by what Indians out-fielder? (Hint: For just one season, he, too, looked like a "natural.") Answer: Joe Charboneau, who appeared as a member of the New York Knights baseball team.

66 **Nicknames:** Dennis "El Presidente" Martinez, P, 1994-1996. A mainstay of the pitching staff in the 1995 season. Dennis was given this title by teammates for his political involvement in his native Nicaraugra. He showed great pitching leadership during his tenure in Cleveland.

67 **Indians MVP:** Lou Boudreau (1938–1950) was the team's player-manager from 1942 to 1950. He was named the American League's Most Valuable Player in the Tribe's world championship year of 1948. As the shortstop and team manager, Lou batted .355, hit 18 home runs, batted in 116 runs, and struck out only nine times in 560 at-bats that year.

68 **Rutherford "Chico" Salmon,** utility infielder from 1964 to 1968. One of the more interesting personalities to wear an Indians uniform, Chico was afraid of ghosts and evil spirits. He slept with the lights on, and sometimes left the television on to keep the spirits at bay.

69 **Bad Trade:** Another trade by Frank "Trader" Lane. This one positively makes Tribe fans buckle at the knees and collapse in fits of rage. On June 15, 1958, Lane, the Tribe's general manager, traded slugging outfielder Roger Maris, pitcher Dick Tomanek, and first baseman Preston Ward to the Kansas City Athletics for first baseman Vic Power and shortstop Woody Held. Maris was then traded to the New York Yankees in 1959; Power and Held did have productive careers in Cleveland. But the baseball world will always remember that, in 1961, Maris broke Babe Ruth's single-season home run record by clubbing 61 round-trippers. Lane later contended it was the best deal he ever made for the Indians.

70 **The Gordon Cobbledick Golden Tomahawk Award:** This annual honor is named for *The Plain Dealer*'s legendary sports editor Gordon Cobbledick and is voted by the players in recognition of the team's outstanding player of the year. Since 1963, multiple award winners have been Andre Thornton (1978, 1979, 1983), Joe Carter (1986, 1988), Carlos Baerga (1991, 1992), and Albert Belle (1993, 1995).

71 **Indians Books:** *Cleveland Baseball* (Timewise Publishers of Lakewood, 1995). Updated annually, this is the best prescription for Cleveland fans requiring an infusion of stats.

72 **Perfection:** On May 15, 1981, a cool, drizzly evening at Municipal Stadium, Indians pitcher Len Barker set down 27 Toronto Blue Jays in a row before 7,290 anxious fans. Barker got excellent fielding support from shortstop Tom Veryzer, second baseman Duane Kuiper, and center fielder Rick Manning to ensure the perfect game (a 3–0 win), the second in Tribe history, and the Indians' fifteenth no-hitter.

Barker hurls perfect game

73 **Player-Manager:** A reserve catcher for the Indians in 1962–1963, Doc Edwards returned in 1987 to take over for fired manager Pat Corrales halfway through the season. He was replaced as manager late in the 1989 season by John Hart.

74 **Gaylord Perry's consecutive victories streak.** Gaylord was in hot pursuit of the Johnny Allen's American League record of 17 consecutive wins when he faced the Oakland A's on July 8, 1974, seeking his own sixteenth victory in a row. The Tribe lost a heartbreaker in Oakland, 4–3, and Gaylord took his place behind Allen. The excitement of this game was so intense in Cleveland that local television station WJW-TV (Channel 8) arranged for a special late-night hookup to televise the West Coast game back to Cleveland.

75 **Herb Score-ism:** One of Herb's broadcast partners remarked that an opposing batter had hit 19 times in 42 at-bats against the Tribe during a season, to which Herb replied, "I'm no good at math, but even I know that's over .500!"

76 **Indians Record:** On July 31, 1963, the Indians set a club record with four consecutive home runs in a single inning, when Woodie Held, Pedro Ramos, Tito Francona, and Larry Brown hit roundtrippers against the Los Angeles Angels.

77 **Great Expectations:** In 1963, the Indians counted on rookie shortstop Tony Martinez (1963–1966) to continue performing as he did in the minor leagues and revive the sagging Tribe. Tony didn't come close to the predictions of stardom, however, hitting an anemic .156 in 1963. He was benched in May 1963 and appeared in only 73 games during his stint with the Tribe.

78 **Not-So-Perfect:** On the receiving end of a home run barrage was Indians pitcher Cal McLish on May 22, 1957, at Fenway Park. Cal gave up four home runs in the sixth inning to Red Sox batters Gene Mauch, Ted Williams, Dick Gernert, and Frank Malzone.

79   **TV broadcasters Harry Jones and "Mudcat" Grant.** From 1973 to 1977, former Indians pitcher Jim "Mudcat" Grant would butcher the names of players and cities alike, welcoming fans from "Book-a-rus" (Bucyrus, Ohio), "Ma-silly-on" (Massillon, Ohio), "Fostor-rea" (Fostoria, Ohio) and pronouncing third baseman Toby Harrah's name as Toby "Hurrah." Harry Jones often sat in stunned silence at Mud's exquisite enunciations.

80   **Tribe Top 10:** Indians career leaders in games played (through the 1997 season): Terry Turner, 1619 (1904–1918); Napoleon Lajoie, 1,614 (1902–1914); Lou Boudreau, 1,560 (1938–1950); Jim Hegan, 1,526 (1941–1942, 1946–1957); Tris Speaker, 1,519 (1916–1926); Ken Keltner, 1,513 (1937–1944, 1946–1949); Joe Sewell, 1,513 (1920–1930); Earl Averill, 1,509 (1929–1939); Charley Jamieson, 1483 (1919–1932); Jack Graney, 1402 (1908, 1910–1922); (Of course, free agency has doomed numbers like these!)

Recollections . . .

Matt Underwood, WEWS-TV sports director, recalls a memorable moment early in his career as a sports broadcaster:

"1995 was a magical year. One event stands out for me. I was doing the postgame interview for the Indians radio network and was trying to grab the hero of the game for an interview after the first game of the Division Series against the Red Sox. It went into extra innings and Albert Belle tied it in the bottom of the eleventh inning with a solo home run to make it 4–4. For sure Belle would be my postgame interview. No…Maybe one of the Tribe pitchers—Martinez, Plunk, Tavarez, or Mesa. I searched the scorecard furiously to select the right player. Then in the bottom of the 13th inning with a cool light rain falling on this late-night game, my unsuspecting hero emerged. With two outs and a 3–0 count, reserve catcher Tony Pena went back on his heels and sent a shot into the left-field bleachers to win the game 4–3. As I interviewed Tony, his smile spread from ear to ear. He said it was one of the most exciting moments of his career. I know it was one of mine!"

81 **Indians Luck:** On April 3, 1966, the Cleveland Indians, Philadelphia Phillies, and New York Mets participated in a lottery for the rights to a University of Southern California pitcher who had been declared ineligible for college baseball after signing illegally with the Atlanta Braves. The Mets won the lottery and the rights to Tom Seaver, who went on to a brilliant career.

82 **Relief pitchers entering the game at Cleveland Municipal Stadium.** Until the late 1970s, relievers were driven in an automobile from the outfield bullpen, around the Stadium track, to the front of their dugout.

83 **Sports Illustrated Covers:** "Sudden" Sam McDowell—billed as "Faster than Koufax"—was the coverboy on *SI*'s May 23, 1966, issue.

84

Nicknames: Al "Senor" Lopez, Manager, 1951–1956. Lopez holds the best winning percentage for any Cleveland manager, .617 (570 wins, 354 losses). He guided the Indians to five second-place finishes and a berth in the 1954 World Series. After the Indians lost four straight games to the New York Giants in the 1954 World Series, Lopez was as surprised (and disappointed) as everybody else: "They say anything can happen in a short series. I just didn't expect it to be that short."

85

Opening Day: In what *Plain Dealer* sports editor Hal Lebovitz called "a storybook debut," Cleveland's Frank Robinson hit a dramatic home run in his first at-bat as the team's new player-manager before 56,715 Opening Day fans at Cleveland Stadium on April 8, 1975. The Indians went on to defeat the New York Yankees 5–3.

56,204 see Robby's storybook debut

86 **Indians Hall of Famer:** Pitcher Bob Feller played for Cleveland from 1936 to 1956 (except during World War II, when he served in the military). One of the greatest pitchers in the history of the game, Bob holds most of the Indians' pitching records, including most victories (266), most no-hitters (3), most one-hit games (12), and most strikeouts (2,581). He was inducted at Cooperstown in 1962.

87 **The Chief Wahoo caricature** on *The Plain Dealer's* front page the morning after a game, from the late 1940s through the 1960s. Tribe fans instantly knew the outcome of a game just by the physical condition of the Chief. A day game victory saw a smiling Wahoo; a night game victory saw Wahoo with the same grin holding a lantern; two fingers up denoted a doubleheader victory. Defeats saw the Chief being clubbed over the head with a bat, while a doubleheader split had Wahoo half-cheerful, half-beaten.

INDIANS MEMORIES

88   **A Fan Favorite:** As part of the major league's 1976 salute to the nation's Bicentennial, baseball fans were asked to vote for their team's most memorable moment in history. Tribe fans picked a rather recent moment: player-manager Frank Robinson's dramatic home run against the New York Yankees on April 8, 1975.

89   **Indians Record:** The record for most home runs hit by a Tribe batter in one game was set by Rocky Colavito (1955–1959, 1965–1967) when he slammed four homers against the Orioles at Baltimore's Memorial Stadium on June 10, 1959.

Colavito Slams 4 Homers; Tribe Wins

Recollections . . .

Karl Bunkleman, Indians bat boy wanna-be, Euclid, Ohio.

"In 1957, I entered The Plain Dealer's essay contest to become a bat boy for the Indians. I didn't win the contest, but I did secure an 'alternate' job as a 'ball boy' in foul territory down the third base line at Municipal Stadium. One important rule was to grab your chair and get out of the way if a play on a foul ball was made near you. In a game against New York, a Yankee foul pop representing the third out came my way. In baseball lingo, it 'froze' me and Indians third baseman Al Smith ran into me, missing the ball, thus extending the inning. The Yankees scored in that inning and went on to beat the Tribe. After the game, I received some personal instructions from manager Kerby Farrell. I cannot repeat these instructions where young children might read them, except to say I was asked to leave the clubhouse and never come back."

90 **The Winning Streak of 1966.** Hopes were sky-high in Cleveland when the Tribe started the 1966 season with 10 straight victories and went 14-1 in the first 15 games. But by season's end, they were at an all-too-familiar 81 wins and 81 losses. Manager Birdie Tebbetts was fired on August 18, 1966, and replaced by George Strickland.

91 **Family Affair:** Tito and Terry Francona both played for the Indians as first basemen–outfielders. Tito (John) played from 1959 to 1964, and son Terry called the Wigwam home for only one season in 1988.

92 **Nicknames:** Ken "the Hawk" Harrelson, OF, 1969–1970. One look at the profile of this flamboyant slugger's face and the resemblance was obvious. Ken was acquired from the Red Sox on April 7, 1969, at the start of the season. His 30 home runs for Cleveland that year gave rise to hopes of Ken carrying the 1970 Indians season until . . .

93 **Indians Luck:** On March 19, 1970, in an exhibition game with the Oakland A's, Ken Harrelson broke his leg sliding into second base. "The Hawk" played in only 17 games in 1970, and stayed just one more season with the Tribe.

94 **Opening Day:** In 1974, too help prop up sagging attendance, Indians management hired the "Great Hugo Zucchini" to blast out of a cannon and shoot across the outfield at Municipal Stadium. Hugo didn't help. The Tribe lost, 6–4 to the Milwaukee Brewers.

95 **Memorable Game:** The Tribe game at Cleveland Municipal Stadium was a 4–0 loss to the Chicago White Sox in front of 72,390 fans on October 3, 1993. It was a truly memorable occasion, as former Indians Bob Feller, Mel Harder, Al Rosen, and Bob Lemon came to bid a fond farewell to the lakefront stadium that served as a baseball park for 61 years. Bob Hope, who entertained an Indians crowd in 1947 and had owned a small share of the team during that era, returned in 1993 to sing "Thanks for the Memories."

A loss to remember

96 **Herb Score-ism:** An Indians pitcher on the mound had just walked three consecutive batters to load the bases. Informing the listening audience of this unfortunate event, Herb exclaimed, "Oh my! The Indians just walked the bases loaded on ten straight pitches!"

97 **Pete Franklin's "funeral services" for the Indians** during the late 1960s, '70s, and '80s. When the Tribe went into their annual "June Swoon," Pete would eulogize the team on the air and bury them for the season. Fans sent sympathy cards to the Indians front office personnel and players alike.

98 **Good Trade:** On December 9, 1981, the Indians actually made a trade that helped them, acquiring pitcher Rick Sutcliffe and second baseman Jack Perconte from the Los Angeles Dodgers for pinch hitter Jorge Orta and two minor leaguers. Sutcliffe had been the NL Rookie of the Year in 1979 and went on to pitch very well for the Indians, winning 14 games against eight losses in 1982. He was traded to the Chicago Cubs in 1984. Orta did not impress anyone with the Dodgers.

99 **Tribe Trivia:** What Indians catcher is the only player in major league history to have caught two perfect games? He caught Lenny Barker's 1981 perfect game. Answer: Ron Hassey (1978–1984), who also served as Dennis Martinez's battery mate in his perfect game as a Montreal Expo in 1991.

100 **20-Game Winner:** The 1970, the Tribe finished the season at 76–86. Twenty of those wins belonged to left-hander Sam McDowell, who finished the year with 20 wins and 12 losses.

101 **Memorable Game:** Game 3 of the 1996 American League Division playoffs against the Baltimore Orioles at Jacobs Field on October 4, 1996. The Indians took the lead when, with the count two balls and two strikes, Belle hit a grand slam into the left-field bleachers off Orioles fireball relief pitcher Armando Benitez in the seventh inning. Pandemonium broke out, as the Tribe went on to win. Unfortunately, the Tribe was eliminated from the playoffs the following day.

102 **Player-Manager:** On September 12, 1974, the Indians acquired out-fielder Frank Robinson from the California Angels. A player destined for the Hall of Fame, Frank played only 15 games for the Tribe before being named the team's player-manager on October 3, 1974. In doing so, Robinson became the first African American manager in major league baseball history. He became the full-time manager in 1976 but was fired during the 1977 season. Robinson was inducted into the Hall of Fame in 1982.

103 **"Wow!"** Oakland A's relief pitcher Dennis Eckersley's disbelief was clearly visible when he mouthed the word after watching Tribe out-fielder Manny Ramirez blast a game-winning homer high into the Jake's left-field bleachers on July 16, 1995.

104 **Sports Illustrated Covers:** Herb Score was featured on the May 30, 1955, cover of *SI* as the "Big New Indian."

Recollections . . .

Slider, the Indians colorful—if not graceful—mascot, looks back at a serious but memorable time in his pink, fuzzy career:

"I'll never forget the great time I was having at the American League Championship in 1995. I was dancing along the right-field wall at Jacobs Field in Game 4 waving to all my friends when all of a sudden I was laying on the warning track in right field. Oh, did my leg hurt bad! The Indians' trainers took me to the hospital right away. The nurses weren't used to seeing someone like me, but, along with the doctors, they fixed me up just fine. What I really remember were all the get-well cards sent by the fans. They even sent me pairs of crutches painted in different colors. All the moms were calling Jacobs Field to see if I was okay, 'cause their kids were worried about me. I was in the hospital for one night, but I went right back to Jacobs Field on crutches to cheer for the Indians in the World Series."

105 **Spring Training in Tucson.** For 46 years (1947–1992), Tucson, Arizona, was home to the Tribe's "Cactus League" spring training. The Indians played their games at Hi Corbett Field and made frequent trips into northern Mexico for exhibition games.

106 **Nicknames:** Phil "Knucksie" Niekro, P, 1986–1987. The crafty knuckleball pitcher shored up a shaky Tribe pitching staff for two seasons.

107 **Good Trade:** On December 10, 1976, the Indians traded pitcher Jackie Brown to the Montreal Expos for first baseman Andre Thornton. One of Cleveland's better swaps. Thornton played first base for three seasons, served as the designated hitter from 1981 to 1987, gained All-Star berths in 1982 and 1984, and earned the Comeback Player of the Year Award in 1982 by hitting 32 home runs with 116 runs batted in. Andre's accomplishments on the field were only surpassed by his team leadership on and off the field.

108 **20-Game Winner:** 1968 was a promising year for the Tribe, as they finished in third place, with 21 of their 86 victories coming via the right arm of pitcher Luis Tiant, who finished the season 21–9.

109 **Player-Manager:** Ken Aspromonte played second base for the Tribe from 1960 to 1962. He returned to take the reins of the club in 1972 and then stepped down in 1974. When Frank Robinson was acquired late in the 1974 season and seemed destined to become manager, Aspromonte told his team that it looked like "they're not going to hire me for next season, so I guess I've been fired."

110 **Indians MVP:** The 1953 season saw Al Rosen, the Tribe's third baseman, earn the American League's Most Valuable Player Award. He played in every game, batted 599 times, hit 43 home runs, knocked in 145 runs, scored 115 runs, and had a .366 batting average. Had he batted .367, he would have won the Triple Crown—highest batting average, most home runs and most RBIs in a single season.

111 **Youngest Indian:** The youngest player to don a major league uniform for a game was pitcher Bob Feller, who began his Indians career in 1936 at age 17.

112   **Oldest Indian:** The Tribe's oldest-ever player was a pitcher, too. Although many rumors surround the age of pitcher Satchel Paige, the oldest player is Phil Niekro, the knuckleball artist who was *officially* 48 years of age when he pitched for the Tribe in 1987.

113   **The all-red home uniforms** worn by the Tribe during the 1972–1975 seasons. Selected by Jim Stouffer, son of Indians owner Gordon Stouffer, the "fire injun red" jerseys and pants embarrassed players so much that they paid $60 each to obtain a more sedate blue jersey to wear with white pants. First baseman Boog Powell dubbed himself the "world's biggest Bloody Mary" when he wore the all-red uniform.

114   **Jim Thome, fashion plate!** In late August, 1997, Tribe players pulled their socks up over their calves in Thome-like fashion for a game to be played on Jim's birthday. Already in first place but thus far unable to pull away from the pack, the team went on from there to play much better baseball and maintain a comfortable distance from its central division rivals. Players kept the socks worn high into the playoffs and 1997 World Series, not wanting to jinx their newly discovered lucky attire.

115 **Rocco Scotti's powerful rendition of the National Anthem** before many Indians home games at Cleveland Municipal Stadium earned him the Civilian Purple Heart Award for his patriotism. Rocco began his wonderful career at the Stadium in 1974 and wrapped it up in 1993.

116 **Cleveland Municipal Stadium's outfield landscaping.** In 1957, Tribe management thought that planting flowers and shrubbery behind the outfield fence and in front of the bleacher wall would enhance the appearance of the field and attract more fans. Shrubbery is nice, but winning teams are better!

117 **Pitcher Steve Dunning's home run** on September 19, 1972, was the last by an Indians pitcher in a regular-season game. (The designated hitter rule took effect in the American League in 1973). Dunning went deep against Detroit Tigers pitcher Mickey Lolich.

118 **Rocky Colavito's on-deck warmup.** "The Rock" would stretch by holding the bat at the barrel end and the handle, raising it behind his head and holding it behind his chest extended. This maneuver was imitated by many youngsters on Cleveland playgrounds and sandlots in the late 1950s.

119 **"Batting Around"**, a sports column featured in *The Plain Dealer*, 1950s–1970s. Written first by reporter Harry Jones and then by Russ Schneider, "Batting Around" gave Tribe fans interesting bits of information on the team and its players along with the columnist's view of the season.

120 **The first interleague game.** The Indians beat the St. Louis Cardinals 8–3 at Busch Stadium in St. Louis on June 14, 1997. Bartolo Colon was the first Tribe pitcher to bat in a regular season game in 24 years.

121 **Phil Seghi's Pipe.** Seghi, general manager from 1973 to 1984, was never without his pipe, which was usually color coordinated with his outfit. While Seghi's baseball knowledge was never questioned, he was prone to forgetting who the players were, often greeting a pitcher with "How ya doin' slugger?"

122 **Jay Bell's first-pitch home run.** Called up from the minor leagues late in the season, shortstop Bell accomplished the amazing feat of hitting the first major league pitch thrown to him out of the ballpark on September 29, 1986.

123 **Nicknames:** Fred "Wingy" Whitfield, 1B, 1963–1967. Fred had a terribly weak left throwing arm. He didn't really throw the ball; he "winged" it.

124 **Good Trade:** On December 6, 1989, the Indians pulled off one of the more significant swaps in team history. Knowing that slugger Joe Carter did not want to remain in Cleveland, the Tribe brass shipped him to the San Diego Padres for catcher Sandy Alomar, third baseman Carlos Baerga, and outfielder Chris James. This trade laid part of the foundation for the Tribe's success in the mid-1990s. Alomar became the American League Rookie of the Year in 1990, while Baerga provided power, excitement, and team leadership until his trade to the New York Mets in 1996. James played two years in Cleveland until he was traded in 1992.

125 **Indians Books:** *Endless Summers: The Fall and Rise of the Cleveland Indians*, by Jack Torry (Diamond Communications, 1995), traces the history of the once-proud Indians, their decline, and their resurgence as an American League powerhouse. This work is a great piece of investigative journalism and provides the fan with a "behind the scene" history of the Tribe.

Recollections . . .

Joe Charboneau, Indians outfielder–designated hitter (1980–1982) remembers his first Opening Day game in 1980:

"The stands were packed. I got a huge cheer on my first at-bat and hadn't even done anything in Cleveland yet. On my third at-bat I hit a three-run home run. We won the game and I honestly thought that every day would be like that one. That day and that game is my favorite baseball memory."

126   **Player-Manager:** In 1963, the Indians acquired first baseman Joe Adcock from the Milwaukee Braves. Adcock was then traded to the Los Angeles Angels after the end of the season. He returned to the Tribe as manager for the 1967 season, even though he had no previous experience as a manager or coach. Adcock's style was no-nonsense: "Things are going to be different around here. If I see things I don't like, the players are going to think that hell was turned loose backwards." Rocky Colavito described Adcock as the "worst manager I ever played for." Indians general manager Gabe Paul said that Adcock "had no imagination—I saw him throw away a Marilyn Monroe calendar just because it was December 31st."

127   **"What can you write about a thing like this?"**—Indians pitcher Early Wynn's question to Gordon Cobbledick of *The Plain Dealer* after the four game sweep of the Indians by the New York Giants in the 1954 World Series.

128 **Sandy Alomar's incredible season.** What a year 1997 was for the All-Star catcher, who had career highs in all batting categories (.324, 21 home runs, 83 RBIs), put together a 30-game hitting streak (one short of the team record), grabbed the All-Star Game MVP award in his home ballpark, played awesome defense while handling an oft-injured pitching staff, and clubbed numerous key- and game-winning hits during season, the playoffs, and the 1997 World Series.

INDIANS 8 *Playoffs '97* **ORIOLES 7**

ALOMARvelous!

129 **Indians Headdress:** In 1951, fans saw the introduction of a new look for Indians caps—now all navy blue with a cartoon version of Chief Wahoo inside a red wishbone "C".

130 **Nicknames:** Harold "Gomer" Hodge, rookie 1971. Harold was dubbed "Gomer" by his Tribe teammates because his speech resembled that of actor Jim Nabors's "Gomer Pyle" character. He also had a Gomer-ish optimism when it came to calculating his batting average. After his fourth pinch hit in four at-bats to start the 1971 season, Harold declared to local sportswriters, "Golly gee, fellas, I'm hitt'n four thousand!"

131 **Memorable Game:** It had been a hapless and hopeless 41-year journey to the playoffs for the Indians. Not since the 1954 World Series had the Indians appeared in the postseason. On October 3, 1995, the Tribe faced the Boston Red Sox at Jacobs Field in the first game of the American League Divisional Series. In dramatic fashion, the Indians won the 13-inning playoff game on a home run by reserve catcher Tony Peña.

Recollections . . .

Scott Keidel, lifelong Indians fan, Columbus, Ohio.

"I can remember receiving several packs of baseball cards as a party favor at my friend's birthday party in 1959. As we opened the packs to retrieve the bubble gum and see who we got, one of the kids began screaming that he had gotten a Rocky Colavito card. I couldn't believe it. For a Cleveland kid, getting Rocky Colavito in a pack of cards was like Christmas morning, the last day of school, and getting a new bike all rolled into one! I tried to trade, bribe, embarrass, and con that card from the kid, but to no avail. I actually cried on the way home, thinking how bad I wanted Colavito. Several years ago, and a few years older, I bought that card at a baseball card show. Although I have the coveted Colavito in my possession, acquiring it didn't soothe my disappointment of 1959."

132 **Sports Illustrated Covers:** Actor-comedian Bob Hope, a Tribe stockholder, appeared on the June 3, 1963, *SI* cover in a new Tribe "vest-style" uniform. Local punsters derided the new Tribe-wear, joking that players were better off wearing bullet-proof vests if the team didn't improve on its recent dismal finishes in the standings.

133 **A Fan Favorite:** Shortstop Omar Vizquel delighted a throng of 40,000 on Public Square in an end-of-season thank-you speech to fans who had come to salute the Indians great 1995 season. Omar's wit and friendly style warmed the hearts of disappointed Cleveland fans, who were still smarting from the World Series loss to the Atlanta Braves.

134 **Scoreboard fireworks at Municipal Stadium.** After an Indians home run, the scoreboard erupted in an explosion of fireworks, plumes of fire, and blaring trumpets.

135 **Cleveland All-Star Games:** Cleveland was host to the mid-summer classic on July 13, 1954. The American League beat the National League by a score of 11–9 before a record crowd of 68,751. The Tribe's Al Rosen hit two home runs, giving the home crowd a thrill. Indians' All-Stars Bobby Avila, Larry Doby, and Bob Lemon also saw playing time. Mike Garcia also represented the Indians but did not play.

CLEVELAND PLAIN DEALER

111TH YEAR—NO. 164　　CLEVELAND, WEDNESDAY MORNING, JULY 14, 1954.　　44 PAGES　　SEVEN CENTS　FINAL

A. L. WINS ALL-STAR GAME, 11-9

136 **Tribe Trivia:** What Indians player was the first major leaguer in history to homer as a right-handed hitter *and* a left-handed hitter in the same inning of a game? Answer: Carlos Baerga, on April 8, 1993 against Yankees pitchers Steve Howe and Steve Farr.

137 **Reliever Ted Abernathy's "submarine" style of pitching.** Right-handder Abernathy played for the Indians in 1963 and 1964. His radical pitching style was a precursor to relievers like Kent Tekulve of the Pittsburgh Pirates. It took a toll on the arm, however. Abernathy was out of baseball soon after he left the Tribe.

138 **The Cleveland Indians Hall of Fame,** housed on the main concourse of Cleveland Municipal Stadium from 1952 to 1971. Club memorabilia and busts of enshrined Tribesmen were on display. When the Stadium needed more room on the main concourse, the mementos were moved to the Ohio Baseball Museum in Springfield, Ohio.

139 **Family Affair:** The Brown brothers, Dick and Larry, wore Tribe uniforms at different times. Older brother Dick was a catcher who played for the Indians from 1957 to 1959. Larry was a shortstop from 1963 to 1971.

140 **MVPs.** In 1990, Cleveland Indians fans were asked to select two "most valuable" Indians players (one fielder and one pitcher) from each decade from the turn of the century up to 1989. Do you agree? Remember, it's most valuable, not most popular.

1900–1909 Napolean Lajoie, 2B; Addie Joss, P
1910–1919 Joe Jackson, OF; Stan Coveleski, P
1920–1929 Tris Speaker, OF; George Uhle, P
1930–1939 Earl Averill, OF; Mel Harder, P
1940–1949 Lou Boudreau, SS; Bob Feller, P
1950–1959 Al Rosen, 3B; Bob Lemon, P
1960–1969 Max Alvis, 3B; Sam McDowell, P
1970–1979 Buddy Bell, 3B; Gaylord Perry, P
1980–1989 Joe Carter, OF; Tom Candiotti, P

141 **Nicknames:** Gary "Ding-Dong" Bell, P, 1958–1967.

142 **Bat Day.** The Indians' Bat Day promotion of the 1960s gave every kid age 14 and under a Louisville Slugger baseball bat with a paid admission to a weekend game, usually a Sunday afternoon affair. The following day's *Plain Dealer* always had a photo of thousands of fans in the stands holding up their free bats. Later, because of security concerns, coupons redeemable for bats were given out instead.

143 **The near-fatal collision of outfielder Leon Wagner and shortstop Larry Brown,** Yankee Stadium, May 4, 1966. Wagner was running in to catch a pop fly hit by Roger Maris; Brown was running out into left field. The two collided, and Wagner suffered a broken nose; Brown was hospitalized and missed six weeks of the season.

144 **Bad Trade:** After six years with the Indians, pitcher Jim "Mudcat" Grant was traded to the Minnesota Twins on June 15, 1964, for pitcher Lee Stange and infielder George Banks. Perhaps the Tribe should have practiced a bit more patience, as Grant went on to win 21 games in 1965 plus two games in the 1965 World Series. Stange was traded to the Boston Red Sox in 1966.

145   **Hitting for the Cycle:** The Indians slugging first baseman Tony Horton joined baseball's elite when he singled, doubled, tripled, and homered against the Orioles in Baltimore on July 2, 1970.

146   **The tragic story of Tony Horton.** This power-hitting first baseman was acquired from the Boston Red Sox in 1967 in a trade for Indians pitcher Gary Bell. Horton was thought to have had the potential to be a premier hitter in the big leagues. Well on his way to compiling great hitting statistics, Horton fell victim to the pressure of the pursuit of perfection as a ballplayer. An emotional breakdown forced him from the game at age 25 during the 1970 season.

147   **The return of Rocky Colavito.** In 1965, this fan favorite led the American League in runs batted in with 108. The Indians drew 281,493 more fans to the Stadium than in 1964.

148   **20-Game Winner:** In his first year in a Tribe uniform, Dick Donovan hit the magical 20-victory mark after coming to Cleveland in a trade with the Washington Senators. Donovan's 20-10 record made him the ace of the Cleveland pitching staff in 1962.

149 **Indians Luck:** After the 1982 season, Indians manager Dave Garcia was fired, and the Tribe brass hired New York Yankee coach Mike Ferraro to take over the job—but only after Yankee manager Billy Martin had turned it down. Ferraro was hired in November 1982, and three months later he underwent surgery to remove a cancerous kidney. During the 1982–1983 off-season, Tribe pitching coach Don McMahon had a heart attack, and third baseman Toby Harrah's house burned down and his father died in a car accident. Having managed a little more than half the season, Ferraro was fired in July 1983 and replaced by Pat Corrales.

150 **The superstitions of Kevin Rhomberg.** Utility infielder Kevin Rhomberg played for the Indians from 1982 to 1984. Among other superstitions, Kevin was fanatical about having to touch a person "last" if he was touched by another person. Teammates would tease him by touching him and then running off, with Kevin in hot pursuit.

Recollections . . .

Ted Bonda, Indians executive vice president (1973–1976) and president (1977–1978), recalls the night of Dennis Eckersley's 1977 no-hitter, May 30, 1977. The Tribe beat the California Angels 1–0.

"Cleveland is a town that loves winners. When I was president of the club, we didn't do a whole lot of that, but one night, one winning night, I'll never forget. Early in the 1977 season, Dennis Eckersley pitched a fantastic no-hitter against the California Angels at the Stadium. The whole team was so excited in the dressing room after the game, that I guess I got caught up in it, too. I gave Dennis a raise that night for his no-hitter, even though I knew we couldn't afford it. On that night, baseball was fun."

151 **Straight A's.** Did you get straight A's in the 1950s, 1960s, or 1970s? If you did, chances are you took your report card downtown to the *Cleveland Press* and received tickets to an Indians games. The tickets were usually for seats in the outfield or the upper deck, but that didn't matter—you were going to Cleveland Stadium to see an Indians game!

152 **Nicknames:** Barry "Shoulders" Latman, P, 1960–1963. His shoulders were the widest part of his physique. Latman was the player received from the Chicago White Sox in exchange for Herb Score in 1960.

153 **Ouch!:** On May 26, 1993, as the Indians played the Texas Rangers at Municipal Stadium, Tribe batter Carlos Martinez launched a high drive to right field. As Ranger outfielder Jose Canseco went airborne to make the catch, the ball went through his glove, hit him on the head, and bounced over the fence for a round-tripper. Canseco's commentary on his painful blooper?: "I'll be on ESPN for a month!"

154 **Gorman Thomas,** who spent only one season with the Indians, as an outfielder in 1983, occupied many different lockers in the Indians clubhouse at Cleveland Municipal Stadium. Not wanting to be noticed, Thomas moved around until he landed in a tiny locker in the far corner of the dressing room where hardly anyone could see him.

155 **The "Albert Shuffle."** One of outfielder Albert Belle's superstitions was to stutter-step before each base in his home run trot. In Belle's Indians career (1989–1996), he performed the shuffle 242 times to become the Tribe's career home run leader.

156 **Player-Manager:** George Strickland had two stints with the Tribe as a shortstop/third baseman in 1952–1957 and 1959–1960. He was thrust into the manager's job in 1966 when manager Birdie Tebbetts suffered a heart attack during spring training. George led the team to a 15–24 season start.

157   **Herb Score-ism:** "There's a sharp drive to the outfield . . . no, it's caught by the shortstop for an out."

158   **Indians Record:** The most fans to click the turnstiles in a single season occurred at Jacobs Field during the 1996 season. 3,318,174 fans saw their Indians try to get back to the World Series after the miraculous 1995 season. At Municipal Stadium, 2,620,627 fans watched the Tribe during the 1948 championship season.

159   **Nicknames:** Joe "Flash" Gordon, 2B, 1947–1950. Taken from the movie character, this nickname was appropriate for Gordon, who was quick and flashy in his own right when playing the infield for the Tribe.

160   **20-Game Winner:** 1956 was the year for young Indians pitcher Herb Score. After an impressive rookie season in 1955, Herb achieved a 20 and 9 record in 1956. Pitching mates Bob Lemon and Early Wynn were also 20-game winners that year.

161   **Bad Trade:** On April 7, 1969, the Indians thought they had traded for a star player and come out even on pitching. In exchange for pitchers Sonny Siebert and Vincente Romo and catcher Joe Azcue, the Tribe obtained first baseman/outfielder Ken Harrelson and pitchers Dick Ellsworth and Juan Pizzaro. Harrelson broke his leg at the beginning of the 1970 season, and Ellsworth and Pizarro didn't help the Tribe. Siebert, however, was a consistent pitcher for Boston, winning 57 games over the next four years, and Romo pitched well in relief.

162   **Speaking of Joe Azcue and Sonny Siebert . . .** They were involved in one peculiar, if not near disastrous event. In a game during the 1966 season, Azcue hit Siebert in the back of the head while trying to throw out a base runner attempting to steal second base. No harm done, but the runner was safe.

163   **Indians Record:** Only 562,507 showed up at cavernous Municipal Stadium to watch the 1963 Indians season, setting the record for lowest attendance in the modern era of Tribe baseball. That was equal to about eight Browns home-game crowds

164 **Eat your Wheaties?** Indians relief pitcher José Mesa and outfielder Kenny Lofton appeared on the front of the Wheaties cereal box at the conclusion of the 1995 season. General Mills, the cereal's producer, honored the Tribe for their 1995 American League Championship.

165 **Nicknames:** Lou "Sweet Lou" Johnson, OF/PH, 1968. His smooth style earned him the nickname and apparently helped him in other areas of his life. On the last day of the 1968 season, he asked a local Cadillac dealer if he could test drive a Coupe de Ville. Lou "tested" it all the way home to Los Angeles.

166 **No-Hitter:** The championship season of 1948 was doubly special for Tribe pitcher Bob Lemon, as he tamed the Detroit Tigers on June 30, 1948, in Tiger Stadium. The Indians won 2–0. It was Lemon's first and only no-hitter.

167 **Indians Luck:** In 1973, Indians general manager Gabe Paul had "unbreakable" plexiglass installed in the press box at Municipal Stadium. Ironically, in the third inning of the inaugural game for the new windows, a foul ball broke through the glass and hit Paul in the head.

Recollections . . .

Sam McDowell, Indians pitcher (1961–1971), recalls the 1966 season.

"Back when I pitched for the Indians, not all major league teams had the television coverage they have today. The Indians were rarely on network television because nobody really wanted to see us play. During the 1966 season, I had pitched back-to-back one-hit games. We were headed to Chicago to play the White Sox, and if I pitched a third straight one-hit game I'd break the record for consecutive one-hitters. Well, the national networks wanted to cover my game against the White Sox on the chance I'd break the record. My pregame routine was never to give an interview immediately before a game. However, the great Dodger pitcher Sandy Koufax was working as a broadcaster for NBC and asked if he could interview me before we took the field. Because it was Sandy, I made an exception and agreed to it. To this day, relatives who tuned in a little late to the game wondered why I wasn't pitching. It was because I faced the first nine batters without an out and was removed from the game in the first inning. You can bet I never gave an interview right before a game ever again!"

168 **No-Hitter:** Dennis Eckersley, the fire-balling righthander, threw his first (and the Tribe's 14th) no-hitter on May 30, 1977, beating the California Angels 1–0. More remarkable, Eckersley did not allow a hit in the last 7-2/3 innings of his previous start on May 25, 1977, and pitched no-hit ball for 5-2/3 innings in his next start on June 5, 1977. That's 22-1/3 hitless innings, two outs short of Cy Young's major league record.

169 **Journeyman pitcher Dennis Higgins,** disgusted at being yanked from a game by manager Alvin Dark during the 1970 season, threw his mitt into the stands as he approached the dugout. Presumably because of fans' disgust with the Tribe that year, the mitt was thrown back onto the field.

170 **Indians Books:** *Day by Day in Cleveland Indians History*, by Morris Eckhouse (Leisure Press, 1983). Although this work covers the events surrounding the Tribe through the 1982 season, it is a masterpiece of detail. Eckhouse does his usual expert job of supplying Tribe fanatics with information on trades, statistics, and history.

171 **One-Game Wonder:** Actually, Indians coach Mel Harder managed the team for three games on an interim basis. On October 1, 1961, he piloted the Tribe to an 8–5 win over the Los Angeles Angels after manager Jimmy Dykes was fired. Mel answered the call again on September 30, 1962, when manager Mel McGaha was dismissed. He guided the Indians to a doubleheader sweep, again over the Los Angeles Angels.

172 **Nicknames:** "Eatin' Ed" Farmer, P, 1971–1973. During his career, Farmer was thrown out of several all-you-can-eat restaurants in American League cities.

173 **Original Indians "bobbin' head" dolls,** featuring the likeness of Indians mascot Chief Wahoo. Now more than 30 years old, these novelty items can fetch hundreds of dollars at sports memorabilia shows.

174 *Wahoo! What a Finish!,* **the Indians 1995 highlight film,** details the excitement of the 1995 American League champs and their frantic finishes in more than just a few games.

175 **Rookie of the Year:** The surprise of 1980 had to be the Indians' "Super Joe" Charboneau, the slugging outfielder from the farm system. He hit the Cleveland scene with a big bat and a Bunyan-like reputation for boxcar boxing matches, extracting his own teeth, drinking beer through his nose, and swallowing raw eggs, shell and all. He hit 23 home runs, batted in 87 runs, and finished the year with a .289 batting average. Though dubbed "Super Joe" by baseball writer Terry Pluto, Charboneau sustained a back injury, and his career went quickly downhill.

176 **Nicknames:** Rico "Big Mon" Carty, OF/1B, 1974–1977. At 6'4" and with a deep baritone voice, Rico gave himself this nickname as a self-appointed leader of the team. Rico often took younger players under his wing as they learned what life in the big leagues was all about.

177 **Joe Earley Night at Cleveland Municipal Stadium.** During the 1948 season, a fan by the name of Joe Earley wrote a letter to the *Cleveland Press* pointing out the need for fan recognition. Indians owner Bill Veeck decided to honor Joe as the typical fan from the 1948 season. Before the game on September 28, 1948, the Indians presented Joe with a new car, refrigerator, and washing machine.

Recollections . . .

Tony Rizzo, sports broadcaster, WMJI-FM 105.9 and WJW-TV8, recalls the long-term influence of being an Indians fan:

"I'll never forget being led up the long ramp at Cleveland Stadium by my dad when I was six years old and then seeing this huge green outfield with players that seemed bigger than life and so mechanical. To a small kid, their hitting, throwing, and fielding was so perfect, so fast, and so strong that I decided that's what I was going to be—a major league baseball player, hopefully with my Indians. Although I didn't make it, I am fortunate to be covering baseball and other sports in Cleveland and getting to live parts of my dream by being close to the baseball team I idolized when I first started going to Indians games with my dad. I'm convinced the reason I work in the field of sports today is due, in large measure, to my desire as a kid to become a professional ball player."

178 ***The Plain Dealer's* Bat Boy Contest.** Actually, the winner of the essay contest sponsored by *The Plain Dealer* became the bat boy for the visiting team and then moved to the Indians clubhouse the following year. Each winter, thousands of eager participants honed their writing skills in hopes of being chosen as the Indians bat boy.

179 **No-Hitter:** Five years after his second no-hitter and 11 years after his first, Bob Feller made baseball history again on July 1, 1951, as he held the Detroit Tigers hitless in a game at Cleveland Municipal Stadium. Errors and a sacrifice fly enabled the Tigers to score a run, but the Tribe won 2–1. It was the eleventh no-hitter in Cleveland history.

180 **"Most Memorable Personality":** A fan poll conducted by the Indians in 1975 selected Rocky Colavito as the Indians all-time "most memorable personality."

181 **Memorable Game:** Another gem from the 1995 season saw the Tribe come from behind against the California Angels on July 18 at Jacobs Field. In what many fans consider the most dramatic finish of the season, Albert Belle lifted the Tribe to a victory. Trailing 5–3 in the bottom of the ninth, Belle stepped up to the plate to face one of the best relievers in recent baseball history, Lee Smith. Great pitcher vs. great hitter, bases loaded. The matchup had the makings of high drama. It did not disappoint, as Belle crushed a Lee Smith slider into the picnic area beyond the center field wall for a grand-slam home run. Final score: Indians 7, California 5.

Tribe enjoys a late feast

Belle wins it with grand slam into picnic tables

182   **Better Late Than Never.** The Tribe reaped the benefits of several Hall of Fame players late in their careers. Ralph Kiner, outfielder for the Pittsburgh Pirates and Chicago Cubs (1946–1954), stopped in Cleveland in 1955 and was inducted in 1975. Pitcher Hal Newhouser spent two years in Cleveland (1954–1955) after a career in Detroit (1939–1953) and was enshrined in 1992. Steve Carlton pitched in 23 games for Cleveland in 1987 after stops with the St. Louis Cardinals, Philadelphia Phillies, San Francisco Giants, and Chicago White Sox (1965–1986); he was enshrined in 1994. Phil Niekro pitched for the Atlanta Braves and New York Yankees (1964–1985), and for the Tribe in 1986–1987; he entered Cooperstown in 1997.

183   **Cleveland All-Star Games:** On July 9, 1963, Cleveland Municipal Stadium hosted the sole midsummer classic after four years of two All-Star games per season. 44,160 fans took in this afternoon game and saw the National League's Willie Mays lead his team to a 5–3 win over the American League.

184 **Nicknames:** Jerry "Dibber" Dybzinski, SS, 1980–1982. The nickname was an obvious play on his last name. Jerry, a native Clevelander, could be recognized by his bow-legged batting stance.

185 **Hitting for the Cycle:** Indians center fielder Larry Doby did it against the Braves in Boston on June 4, 1952.

186 **Memorable Game:** In the 1995 American League Championship play-off against the Seattle Mariners, Game 4 in Cleveland was pivotal, as the Tribe was down in the series two games to one. The Indians played without the injured Albert Belle and Sandy Alomar, and even mascot Slider was injured, after slipping off the right-field wall. But, thanks to home runs by Eddie Murray and Jim Thome, the series evened-up at two games each as the Tribe shut-out the Mariners 7–0. This game brought the players and fans back to believing.

187 **The postvictory ritual of Tribe pitcher Luis "Looey" Tiant,** Tribe pitcher from 1964 to 1969. Tiant always lit up a *huge* Cuban cigar. Doesn't sound too odd, except that there was one more important part to the celebration: Luis would shower while puffing away on the stogie, and, according to teammates, the cigar always stayed lit!

188 **Chief Wahoo,** again put in a place of prominence, at the beginning of the 1962 season. With the Gate A Chief Wahoo only a memory, the Tribe brass placed the Chief on Municipal Stadium's roof standing in a batter's pose on the scripted word "Indians." When the team moved to Jacobs Field in 1994, the sign moved to the Western Reserve Historical Society's Reinberger Gallery.

189 **Herb Score-ism:** "There's a two hopper to Vizquel, who fields it on the first bounce."

190 **"Batgate."** The corked-bat incident involving outfielder Albert Belle led to a seven-game suspension for the Indians slugger during the 1994 season. Upon a request by the White Sox that Belle's bat be inspected for an illegal cork center, the umpires placed it in their dressing room at Chicago's Comiskey Park for safe keeping. That night the bat was stolen and replaced with one of first baseman Paul Sorrento's legal bats. With the inept substitution fooling no one, the umpires demanded another of Belle's bats and found it to be corked. Belle claimed that the White Sox had set him up by stealing all his bats and corking them.

191 **20-Game Winner:** Pitcher Early Wynn (1949–1957, 1963) joined the magical 20-game-victory club in 1951 (20 wins, 13 losses), in 1952 (23–12), in 1954 (23–11), and again in 1956 (20–9). Known for his tenacity, Wynn didn't take kindly to hitters who showed him up—or for that matter, to any hitter. Take, for example, his response to rumors that he would knock down his grandmother if she crowded the plate: "Aw, I wouldn't do anything like that—unless it meant winning the game."

192 **Pitcher Jim "Mudcat" Grant's soap uniform.** Before every game he was scheduled to pitch, Grant would rub a bar of soap all over his uniform. Did the "Mudcat" have an aversion to dirt? No. During a game, as he wiped his pitching hand on his uniform, he'd really be greasing his hand with soap in order to help throw a type of spitball. He stopped the practice one hot, sweaty day when his uniform started to bubble.

193 **Indians Record:** Everyone is interested in most home runs, most RBIs, and the most hits in a season, but how about the most strikeouts by a hitter? That dubious honor goes to Indians outfielder Cory Snyder (1986–1990), who went down swinging 166 times in 1987.

194 **Indians Hall of Famer:** Lou Boudreau played for the Tribe from 1938 to 1952, becoming player-manager in 1942 at the age of 24. A very productive hitter and an excellent fielder, the "Boy Manager" led the AL in hitting in 1944 with a .327 average and helped lead Cleveland to a World Championship in 1948, when he was named the American League's Most Valuable Player. He was inducted at Cooperstown in 1970.

Recollections . . .

Cy Buynak, visiting team equipment manager for the Cleveland Indians and home clubhouse manager for the Tribe from 1966–1993.

"The one event that stands out for me is Lenny Barker's perfect game on May 15, 1981. It's one of baseball's greatest achievements that hardly ever happens. The tension started to build in the sixth or seventh inning. I stayed down in the Indians clubhouse and didn't go up to the dugout, which I normally did about the third inning. When a pitcher has a "no-no" going, I stayed with what I was doing in the clubhouse so I wouldn't jinx Lenny. When Rick Manning made the last out, I laid a path of towels from the clubhouse entrance right to Lenny's locker where the champagne was waiting. Although there were only about three thousand people at the game, when you talk to people about the game today, it's like there were 50,000 there that night. Everybody says they were there, but I know I was and it was the greatest!"

195 **Ouch!** Indians' pitcher Bud Black owns the dubious team record for most batters hit in one inning. On July 8, 1988, he hit three Oakland A's in the fourth inning.

196 **Joe Adcock's unusual protest.** As Tribe manager on opening day in 1967, Adcock charged out of the dugout to claim that the new all-white shoes worn by Kansas City were illegal. The protest was thrown out by American League president Joe Cronin the next day.

197 **Nicknames:** Saturnino Orestes Armas Arrieta "Minnie" Minoso, OF, 1949, 1951, and 1958–1959. The name "Minnie" was shorter than all his given names and sounded better, too. Whenever he went into a hitting slump, Minnie would run into the locker room and shower fully clothed, claiming he was "washing away evil spirits." In one particular game, following his shower routine, Minnie collected three hits. After that game, ten of Minnie's teammates showered in their uniforms.

198 **Brook Jacoby,** a solid performer for the Tribe from 1984 to 1992, never washed the favorite shirt he began wearing under his jersey in his rookie year. The third baseman attributed his 1986 All-Star selection to the "strength" of the shirt.

199 **Sports Illustrated Covers:** Albert Belle was featured on May 6, 1996. *SI* examined the explosive outfielder in an article entitled, "Tic-Tic-Tic."

200 **Home games against the Yankees in the late 1950s and early 1960s.** In the 1959 season, with the Indians clinging to first place, the Yanks came to town and won three out of four games in the early June series. Of note was the crowd: 128,914 took in that weekend series, with 59,823 showing up for the Sunday doubleheader. *Cleveland Press* columnist Frank Gibbons commented, "[I]f the Indians did nothing else in this Yankee series, they helped demonstrate that the Cleveland area is still one of the hottest baseball beds in the entire country."

201 **Tribe Trivia:** No player ever hit a home run into the center-field seats in the history of Cleveland Municipal Stadium.

202 The **"Basebelles,"** a group of female Indians fans that organized booster events, luncheons, and behind-the-fence picnics at Cleveland Stadium from the 1960s to the 1980s. Founded by Jessie Semple O'Donnell in 1965, the group did much to support baseball in Cleveland during the Tribe's lean years.

203 **Nicknames:** Rick "Archie" Manning, OF, 1975–1983. Rick was dubbed "Archie" after University of Mississippi and New Orleans Saints quarterback Archie Manning. A back injury in 1977 limited Manning's effectiveness for a time, but his hustle and desire to play the game was always evident. He was traded to the Milwaukee Brewers in 1983. Fans now listen to Rick and broadcast partner John Sanders do the Indians play-by-play on SportsChannel.

204 **The annual "Ribs and Roasts" dinners** sponsored by the Cleveland Chapter of the Baseball Writers Association of America. Usually held at the former Cleveland Sheraton Hotel on Public Square, it featured the Indians Player of the Year Award, a stage full of writers and broadcasters making fools of themselves, and players and front office folks in various songs and skits. Begun in 1947, Ribs and Roasts left the scene in the late 1970s when the Sports Media Association of Cleveland and Ohio (SMACO) took over the annual banquets.

205 **Memorable Game:** In one of the best comebacks in their history, the Indians defeated the Minnesota Twins 11–10 on September 28, 1984. Down by 10 runs in the bottom of the third inning, the Tribe scored two runs in the third inning, seven in the sixth inning, and one run in both the eighth and ninth. The defeat cost the Twins the lead in the American League West Division and eliminated them from the pennant race.

206 **Player-Manager:** As part of the Tribe's "keystone" combination with shortstop Lou Boudreau, second baseman Joe Gordon played for Cleveland from 1947 to 1950. He returned to the Wigwam to manage the Tribe from 1958 to 1960.

207 **Indians Record:** Longest Game, Innings. August 31, 1993 saw the longest game played in terms of innings—22, a 5–4 loss to the Minnesota Twins at the Metrodome in Minneapolis.

208 **Indians Headdress:** Beginning in 1958, the Indians removed the cartoon caricature of Chief Wahoo from the navy-blue cap. The only symbol remaining was the familiar red wishbone "C" outlined in white. Chief Wahoo remained on the sleeve of the uniform.

Recollections . . .

Jim "Mudcat" Grant, Indians pitcher (1958–1964), on Indians Hall of Fame pitcher Satchel Paige:

"Satchel gave me some good advice about pitching in the majors. He said, 'Young man, you've got to have a titty pitch. If you don't have one, you can't win.' I thought he was putting me on, getting ready to say something about sex. He ran his hand over his chest and said, 'A titty pitch is right here.' Of course, he was right—you need to pitch inside to win in this league."

209 **Indians Luck:** In 1971, Indians pitcher Steve Mingori was approaching the team record for game appearances in a season when, on August 4, he was hit in the face during pregame warm-ups by an errant throw. The record was not broken, but Mingori's jaw was.

210 **Bad Trade:** In 1988, the Indians wanted shortstop Julio Franco to switch positions and play second base. Julio wouldn't play along and was traded to the Texas Rangers on December 6, 1988, for first baseman Pete O'Brien, outfielder Odibe McDowell, and second baseman Jerry Browne. Julio had four great years with Texas and won the American League batting title in 1991 with a .341 average. O'Brien left the Tribe after one season, McDowell was traded in 1989 to the Atlanta Braves, and Browne played well for two seasons but became a free agent after 1991.

211

American League Champions: The 1995 Indians won the American League pennant but lost the World Series to the Atlanta Braves, four games to two. Here are the A.L. champs of '95:

Indians roster for the World Series:

Manager: Mike Hargrove
Coaches: Buddy Bell, Luis Isaac, Charley Manuel, Dave Nelson, Jeff Newman, Mark Wiley

#7 Kenny Lofton, CF
#8 Albert Belle, LF
#9 Carlos Baerga, 2B
#10 Alvaro Espinoza, IF
#11 Paul Sorrento, 1B/DH
#12 Jesse Levis, C
#13 Omar Vizquel, SS
#17 Tony Pena, C
#20 Ruben Amaro, OF
#24 Manny Ramirez, RF
#25 Jim Thome, 3B

#32 Dennis Martinez, P
#33 Eddie Murray, 1B/DH
#35 Wayne Kirby, OF
#36 Herbert Perry, 1B/OF
#37 Chad Ogea, P
#38 Eric Plunk, P
#41 Charles Nagy, P
#44 Ken Hill, P
#45 Paul Assenmacher, P
#49 José Mesa, P
#50 Julian Tavarez, P
#54 Mark Clark, P
#55 Orel Hershiser, P
#56 Alan Embree, P
#62 Jim Poole, P

212   **Nicknames:** Charley "Bogalusa Bomber" Spikes, OF, 1973–1977. A promising slugger, Charley got his nickname from his hometown of Bogalusa, Louisiana. One time when he was called to pinch hit, Charley hopped off the dugout bench and hit his head on the ceiling of the dugout, knocking himself out.

213   **Greg Swindell**, left-handed hurler for the Tribe from 1986 to 1991, with a brief stop in the Wigwam in 1996. Known for biting off a different fingernail before he started a game and chewing it throughout the contest, Swindell said he'd "never chew tobacco."

214   **20-Game Winner:** From 1948 to 1959, Edward "Mike" Garcia hurled for the Indians. In two of those seasons, 1951 and 1952, Mike reached the 20-game victory mark, going 20–13 in 1951 and 22–11 in 1952.

Recollections . . .

Pat Rominini, Indians home team bat boy (1997).

"During the 1996 season, I was working as a clubhouse attendant for the Indians. I was invited on a nine-game West Coast road trip in August. I was really excited about going, and as departure day got closer, I could barely stand the anticipation. Since it was my first road trip, some of the guys decided to initiate me by repacking my suitcase with their choice of wardrobe. When I walked into breakfast at the hotel the first morning, I was wearing the short red pants, oversized shoes, and outlandish shirt that I found in my bag. Needless to say, there were quite a few people waiting to greet me in the restaurant. Welcome to the big leagues!"

215 **Rookie of the Year:** In 1990, the Baseball Writers of America had voted unanimously to honor Sandy Alomar, Jr., as the American League's Rookie of the Year. Alomar hit .290, had 66 runs batted-in, and hit nine home runs. He also earned a Gold Glove Award for his exceptional catching and defensive play.

216 **No-Hitter:** Tribe pitcher Sonny Siebert achieved some success as a pitcher with the Indians and Boston Red Sox, but on June 10, 1966, he entered baseball's record books when he pitched a no-hitter against the Washington Senators. The Tribe won 2–0.

217 **Nicknames:** Bob "Rapid Robert" Feller, P, 1936–1956. So nicknamed because of his blazing fastball, Feller entered the majors at age 17. Perhaps the greatest of all Tribe hurlers, when Feller retired after the 1956 season, having won 266 games, lost 162, struck out 2,581 batters, pitched three no-hitters, and shut out opposing teams 46 times.

218 **The Deaths of Pitchers Steve Olin and Tim Crews.** On March 22, 1993, during spring training in Winter Haven, Florida, Olin, Crews, and pitcher Bob Ojeda were involved in a tragic boating accident on Little Lake Nellie. Only Ojeda survived the accident; he returned briefly to pitch for the Indians late in the 1993 season. The tragedy hit the young Indians very hard but brought them closer together as they dedicated the season to the two deceased pitchers.

219 **Tribe broadcaster Jack Graney,** who played outfield for the Indians from 1908 to 1922, apparently opened up new opportunities for hundreds of former athletes that would follow him. He was the first professional athlete to go straight from the playing field to the broadcast booth. He did Indians radio play-by-play for 32 years, ending his broadcast career in 1954.

220 **Nicknames:** Don "the Sphinx" Mossi, P, 1954–1958. A left-handed reliever, Don had a face that was strikingly similar to the ancient Egyptian Sphinx. His large ears added to the resemblance.

221 **(Dysfunctional) Family Affair:** Pitchers Fritz Peterson and Mike Kekich were acquired from the Yankees a year apart—Kekich came in a trade on May 12, 1973, and Peterson came on April 27, 1974. The two pitchers share the distinction of having swapped entire families—wives and children—during the early part of the 1973 season. The Yankees, hoping to avoid potential problems, traded Kekich to the Indians. Kekich was dealt away in the spring of 1974 before Peterson arrived.

222 **Tribe Top 10:** Indians Top Ten in Home Runs: Albert Belle, 242 (1989–1996); Earl Averill, 226 (1929–1939)l; Hal Trosky, 216 (1933–1941); Larry Doby, 215 (1947–1955, 1958); Andre Thornton, 214 (1977–1987); Al Rosen, 192 (1947–1956); Rocky Colavito, 190 (1955–1959, 1965–1967); Ken Keltner, 163 (1937–1944, 1946–1949); Joe Carter, 151 (1984–1989); Woodie Held, 130 (1958–1964)

223 **Eddie Murray's 3,000th Hit.** On June 30, 1995, Eddie knocked a single to right in a 4–1 victory over the Twins at the Metrodome.

224   **Outfielder Alex Cole's protective helmet,** worn when playing center field to avoid injury from misplayed fly balls. Apparently a batting helmet was good luck for Alex, who played for the Tribe from 1990 to 1992. On August 1, 1990, in a game against the Kansas City Royals, he became the first Indian to steal five bases in a single game.

225   **Cleveland Municipal Stadium.** Known informally as "Lakefront Stadium," or simply "the Stadium," and disrespectfully as the "Mistake on the Lake," this mammoth structure was part of an economic development package for downtown Cleveland. It was not built to attract the 1932 Olympics to Cleveland, as sometimes conjectured. The structure was completed on July 1, 1931, and the Tribe played their first game there on July 31, 1932, but did not become full-time tenants until owner Bill Veeck moved them permanently from League Park at the start of the 1947 season. The Indians bid farewell to their home on the lake on October 3, 1993, when they played the last game at Cleveland Municipal Stadium. The Tribe's record at Municipal Stadium was 2,224 wins, 1,951 losses, and 12 ties.

226 **Cleveland All-Star Games:** On August 9, 1981, 72,086 fans packed Cleveland Municipal Stadium and welcomed back major league All-Stars from a 50-day player strike. While the city was deprived of much of the hoopla surrounding the midsummer classic because of the strike, the game was close and exciting—the National League edged the American League 5–4. Cleveland's Lenny Barker pitched two innings before the home crowd, and Tribe catcher Bo Diaz tossed a throw into center field while attempting to throw out a base runner.

227 **Family Affair:** Avid Indians fans remember Earl Averill, the Hall of Famer who roamed center field for the Tribe from 1929 to 1939. Earl's son Earl Averill, Jr., played third base and caught for the Indians in 1956 and 1958.

228 **Herb Score-ism:** "There's a long fly ball hit down the right field line. Is it a fair ball? Is it foul? Yes, it is!"

Indians Luck: The 1986 season saw the Tribe post their best record since 1968, winning 84 games and losing 78. They finished 11 1/2 games behind the American League East champion Red Sox. Even the folks at *Sports Illustrated* got into the act: their 1987 preseason baseball issue they featured Indians Cory Snyder and Joe Carter on the cover, stating, "Indian Uprising. Believe it! Cleveland is the best team in the American League!" The Tribe went 61–101 in 1987 and finished 37 games behind the A.L. East champion Detroit Tigers.

229

Player-Manager: Lou Boudreau was possibly the best shortstop the Indians ever had, and some argue that he may have been the best manager as well. Boudreau played for the team from 1938 to 1941 and was the player-manager from 1942 to 1950. In the beginning, reaction to his double duty was not positive. As Franklin "Whitey" Lewis of the *Cleveland Press* wrote on November 25, 1941, "Newspaper comment throughout the nation was bitter or facetious, in spite of the general acceptance of Lou's appointment in Cleveland. The only complaints heard were in the form of fears that the worries of managing might hamper Lou's shortstopping."

230

232   **American League Champions.** The 1954 Indians won the American League pennant but lost the World Series to the New York Giants in four straight games, despite winning 111 games in the regular season. Here are the A.L. champs of 1954:

Indians roster for the World Series:

Manager: Al Lopez
Coaches: Tony Cuccinello, Mel Harder, Ralph Kress, Bill Lobe
#1 Bobby Avila, 2B
#2 George Strickland, SS
#3 Dale Mitchell, OF
#4 Jim Hegan, C
#5 Henry Majeski, IF
#6 Bill Glynn, 1B
#7 Al Rosen, 3B
#8 Rudy Regalado, IF
#11 Art Houtteman, P
#12 Don Mossi, P
#14 Larry Doby, CF

#16 Hal Newhouser, P
#17 Dave Philley, RF
#18 Hal Naragon, C
#19 Bob Feller, P
#20 Ray Narleski, P
#21 Bob Lemon, P
#22 Dave Hoskins, P
#23 Vic Wertz, 1B
#24 Early Wynn, P
#25 Mike Garcia, P
#26 Bob Hooper, P
#32 Al Smith, LF
#31 Wally Westlake, OF
#34 Dave Pope, OF

Recollections . . .

Pat Corrales, Indians manager (1983-1987), on why he could have used more talent on the teams he managed:

"Talent always beats experience, because by the time you get experience, the talent's gone."

INDIANS CLINCH PENNANT

231 **Indians Record:** The worst season record for the Indians in the modern era was posted by the 1991 Indians team, which finished the season with 57 wins and 105 losses, a .352 winning percentage.

233 **Memorable Game:** For drama, nothing can top the game-tying pinch hit of player-manager Lou Boudreau against the Yankees on August 9, 1948, in the first game of a doubleheader. Injured the previous Thursday, Boudreau limped from the dugout to home plate in the seventh inning to the ovation of the home crowd as he was announced as the pinch-hitter for outfielder Thurman Tucker. With the bases loaded and the Tribe down 6–4, Boudreau lined a single to center field to tie the game. Final score: Indians 8, Yankees 6.

234 **Nicknames:** Ross "Skuz" Grimsley, P, 1980. Ross refused to bathe or groom himself while he was on a winning streak. His Indians teammates threatened to lose on purpose if he didn't shower.

235 **No-Hitter:** Dick Bosman, a journeyman pitcher who stopped in Cleveland in 1973–1975, held the world champion Oakland A's hitless, beating them 4–0 on July 19, 1974. The game might have been a perfect game, but Bosman committed a fielding error, allowing one Oakland player to reach first base.

Bosman hurls no-hitter over A's

236 **Good Trade:** On December 9, 1977, the Indians' slugging outfielder Charlie Spikes—who had begun to disappoint as a power hitter—was traded to the Detroit Tigers for shortstop Tom Veryzer. Veryzer was the Tribe's starting shortstop through the 1981 season.

237 **20-Game Winner:** Leading the Tribe pitchers in 20-game victory seasons is Bob Lemon, the stellar right-hander who pitched for Cleveland in 1941–1942 and 1946–1958. Lemon achieved 20 or more victories in 1948, 1949, 1950, 1952, 1953, 1954, and 1956.

238 **Tribe Trivia:** What pitcher has started the most Opening Day games in team history? (He also has the most career victories as a Tribe pitcher.) Answer: Bob Feller started seven Opening Day games for the Tribe.

239 **"Take Me Out to the Ballgame,"** played by saxophonist Maurice ("The Sax Man") Reedus, Jr., on the East Ninth Street approach to Jacobs Field. A fixture for all home games since the ballpark opened in 1994, Maurice, always decked out in Indians cap and sunglasses, entertains before and after the game.

240 **Indians Hall of Famer:** Early Wynn pitched for the Indians from 1949 to 1957 and again in 1963. A hard-nosed pitcher who challenged hitters at the plate, Early garnered 300 victories in his pitching career and won 20 or more games in a season four times. Enshrined in 1972.

241 **The Indians' "Big Four."** The Indians possessed one of the strongest pitching staffs in baseball from 1950 to 1954. The pitching elite of this staff were Bob Feller, Bob Lemon, Mike Garcia, and Early Wynn, who combined for 68 victories in 1950, 79 in 1951, 76 in 1952, 66 in 1953, and 78 in 1954.

242 **Tribe Trivia:** Who is the only major league pitcher to equal his age in number of strikeouts in a nine-inning game? Answer: Bob Feller. In a 5–2 victory over the Detroit Tigers on September 13, 1936, 17-year-old rookie Bob Feller had 17 strikeouts.

243 **Hard-nosed third baseman Toby Harrah,** who played for the Tribe from 1979 to 1983, on his love of baseball: "I'll never quit this game. They'll have to tear the uniform off my back."

244 **Indians Record:** The Tribe has featured some great arms over the years. When it comes to the most game appearances by an Indians pitcher, the record of 582 game appearances is not held by Feller or Lemon but by Mel Harder, the right-hander who pitched for Cleveland from 1928 to 1947.

245 **Opening Day:** On April 13, 1965, Cleveland welcomed back its hero. 44,335 fans turned out for Cleveland's home opener to see slugger Rocky Colavito back in an Indians uniform for the first time since 1959. Rocky hit a home run in the sixth inning as the Tribe defeated the Los Angeles Angels 6–5.

246 **Nicknames:** Jamie "the Rat" Easterly, P, 1983–1987. Jamie's facial features and long mustache gave him a rat-like appearance. "The Rat" once pulled a groin muscle while crossing his legs as he watched television. As a result, he missed several pitching appearances.

247 **Tribe Trivia:** What Indians catcher caught three no-hitters from three different Tribe pitchers? Answer: Jim Hegan, who caught Don Black's no-hitter in 1947, Bob Lemon's in 1948, and Bob Feller's in 1951.

248 **The antics of shortstop Paul Zuvella,** who played with the Tribe briefly in 1988 and 1989. Known as the "stretch master," Zuvella went through an elaborate two-hour stretching regimen before games and between pitches during games. His wild contortions annoyed second baseman Julio Franco to the point where Julio ignored him except during plays.

249 **20-Game Winner:** The career-year of pitcher Gene Bearden was one of the highlights of the 1948 World Series. Gene won 20 games and lost seven. The left-handed knuckleballer beat the Boston Red Sox in the 1948 American League playoff. In the World Series, he pitched a shut-out victory in Game 3.

Recollections . . .

Herb Score, Indians pitcher (1955–1959) and radio voice (1964–1997,), looks back over his longtime association with the game:

"What comes to mind immediately is that I was blessed to have played professional baseball and then move into the broadcast booth when my playing days were over. It's the next best thing to playing. Sure, I have memories of players and games, but I'll remember having my health and the ability to enjoy the game I love and the many fine people I've come to know over the years."

250 **Indians Hall of Famer:** Leroy "Satchel" Paige became a member of the Indians in 1948, having been signed out of the Negro Leagues by Cleveland owner Bill Veeck. Although he played for Cleveland only in 1948 and 1949, Paige is considered by some baseball experts to be among the greatest pitchers of all time. He won 28 games in the majors, after 123 victories in the Negro Leagues. During his 40-year career, it is estimated that he threw in more than 8,000 games. He was inducted at Cooperstown in 1971.

251 **Satchel Paige's Advice on Living:** "Avoid fried meats which angry up the blood. If your stomach disputes you, lie down and pacify it with cool thoughts. Keep the juices flowing by jangling around gently as you move. Go very light on the vices such as carrying on in society—it ain't restful. Avoid running at all times. Don't look back, something might be gaining on you."

252 **Ending Paul Molitor's hitting streak in 1987.** Just as they had done in 1941 against Joe DiMaggio, the Indians ended the 39-game hitting streak of the Milwaukee Brewers' Paul Molitor, who was attempting to tie Ty Cobb's 40-game streak, and reach DiMaggio's record of 56.

253 **Indians Record:** The record for the most home runs hit in a single season is held by Albert Belle, who smashed 50 round-trippers in the 1995 season. He easily surpassed Al Rosen's 1953 total of 43.

254 **Nicknames:** Jerry "the Governor" Browne, 2B, 1989-1990. Jerry, who played second base, had the same name as the former governor of California (but spelled with an "e" on the end).

255 **Player-Manager:** George "Birdie" Tebbetts provided back-up for the Tribe's catcher Jim Hegan. Hired to manage the Indians in 1963, he led them to two fifth-place and one sixth-place finish before being fired on August 18, 1966.

256 **Jacobs Field:** A symbol of the resurrection of the Cleveland Indians' fortunes, Jacobs Field became the home of the Tribe on April 4, 1994, when the team inaugurated the ballpark with a 4–3 Opening Day victory over the Seattle Mariners in front of a capacity crowd of 43,368.

257 **Bad Trade:** Tribe pitcher Dennis Eckersley was traded to the Boston Red Sox for pitchers Rick Wise and Mike Paxton, third baseman Ted Cox, and catcher Bo Diaz on March 30, 1978. Eckersley, one of the Tribe's fine young pitchers, went on to star for the Red Sox and Chicago Cubs, and later found a role as a top relief pitcher with the Oakland Athletics and St. Louis Cardinals. Wise and Paxton were marginal performers for the Indians. Diaz made the All-Star team as an Indian in 1981. Cox was eventually traded to Seattle in 1979.

258 **Nicknames:** Cory "White Knight" Snyder, OF, 1986–1990. Dubbed "White Knight" by manager Pat Corrales in 1987 after his outstanding rookie year of 1986, when he hit 24 home runs and appeared to be one of the noble young rescuers of the Tribe's fortunes. (Cory also had a rather fair complexion.) Cory suffered a tough season in 1987 and was eventually traded to the Chicago White Sox on December 4, 1990.

259 **Great Expectations:** Spring training 1954 saw the phenomenal performance of infielder Rudy Regalado. Filling in at second base for holdout Bobby Avila, Regalado hit 11 home runs and batted .447 prior to Opening day. Manager Al Lopez moved him to third base at the start of the season, but by July Regalado was slumping badly. He hung on with the Tribe in 1955 and 1956, but that was about it. As they say, he was "just a desert mirage."

260 **Max Alvis's bout with spinal meningitis in June 1964.** The Tribe's third baseman (1962–1969) recovered and returned to finish the season. For a time it looked as if the entire Indians team might be quarantined, which would have jeopardized part of the season. The Tribe's schedule continued on without interruption, however, and the team finished in sixth place once again.

261 **Opening Day:** On April 4, 1994, 41,459 fans, including President Bill Clinton (who threw out the first ball), crowded into brand-new Jacobs Field to help usher in a new era of Cleveland Indians baseball. The Tribe faced the Seattle Mariners in a game that nearly went into the record books. The Mariner's Randy Johnson had a no-hitter going until the eighth inning when catcher Sandy Alomar singled. The Tribe tied the game at 2–2 in the eighth, and won the game 4–3 in the eleventh inning when Eddie Murray doubled and came home on a single by Wayne Kirby.

262 **Indians Headdress:** In 1970, the Tribe returned to an all-navy-blue cap with the red wishbone "C" outlined in white. From 1972 through 1977, the navy-blue cap was retained, but a crooked red "C" replaced the conventional lettering of the past.

263 **20-Game Winner:** Bob Feller had six seasons of 20 or more pitching victories: 24–9 in 1939, 27–11 in 1940, 25–13 in 1941, 26–15 in 1946, 20–11 in 1947, and 22–8 in 1951. One wonders what Feller might have achieved if World War II hadn't intervened.

264 **Great Expectations:** Outfielder Charlie Spikes was obtained in a trade with the New York Yankees on November 27, 1972. According to general manager Phil Seghi, Charlie was "going to hit 40–50 home runs a year for a lot of years." After his first two seasons in a Tribe uniform, Spikes lost his edge. He was traded to Detroit in 1977 and was out of baseball by 1980.

265 **Indians Luck:** In 1951, the Indians sold pitcher Sal Maglie to the Brooklyn Dodgers. In 1958, they sold pitcher Hoyt Wilhelm to the Baltimore Orioles. Each player hurled a no-hitter for his new team the very year he was dealt.

266 **The antics of Jimmy Piersall.** Piersall was an outfielder with the Tribe from 1959 to 1961, spending eight years with the Boston Red Sox before coming to Cleveland. Piersall had outrageous arguments with umpires, ran the bases backwards after his 100th home run, and ran back and forth in center field to distract opposing batters. He was the subject of a movie, *Fear Strikes Out* (1957), the story of his recovery from a nervous breakdown in 1952. Anthony Perkins played Piersall.

267 **Tribe Trivia:** Thought of as a shortstop, Lou Boudreau (1938–1950) adorned himself with "the tools of ignorance" and went behind the plate as a catcher several times early in his playing career.

Recollections . . .

Brian Brakeman, fan, Shaker Heights, Ohio.

"There may be substantial debate over the greatest catch by an Indians player. Certainly Kenny Lofton, Larry Doby, and Tris Speaker have contributed to the lore of spectacular fielding. However, there can't be any debate as to who made the best non-catch in Indians history. I will never forget Brad Komminsk, a center fielder for the Indians in 1989, who raced to the center-field wall at Municipal Stadium and literally vaulted over the fence as he made a sensational grab of a sure home run and then disappeared behind the canvas-covered fence. Unfortunately, he dropped the ball while he was behind the fence. With the field umpire checking, Komminsk could not produce the ball in his glove, and the play was quickly ruled a home run."

268 **Emil Bossard, the Indians' venerable groundskeeper.** Emil was hired by the Tribe in 1935 to keep the fields at League Park and Cleveland Stadium in tip-top shape. The legacy of the Bossard family lived on in sons Harold and Marshall, who succeeded their father as Tribe groundskeepers. Emil passed away in 1981 at age 88; Harold retired in 1978, and Marshall hung up his rake in 1985.

269 **Indians Hall of Famer:** Beginning his career as a center fielder, but achieving greatness as a pitcher, Bob Lemon (1946–1958) was enshrined at Cooperstown in 1976. He ranks as one of Cleveland's all-time great pitchers with 207 wins, 128 losses, one no-hitter, and 1,277 strikeouts.

270 **Winning Streaks:** The longest overall consecutive game-winning streak by the Tribe (both home and away) is 13 games. It happened twice: from April 18–May 2, 1942, and again from August 1–14, 1951. The Tribe posted its longest home game winning streak from May 13 to June 19, 1994, when the team won 18 straight at Jacobs Field.

271 **Pitcher Sam McDowell playing second base.** On July 6, 1970, against the Washington Senators, Manager Alvin Dark wanted to keep McDowell, who was pitching, in the game, but Dark didn't want him to face Senators slugger Frank Howard. In a move that surely makes the case for using pencil when keeping score, Dark shifted second baseman Eddie Leon to third base and put McDowell at second. Sam made a putout at second base to end the eighth inning, and finished the game as the pitcher, earning the victory as the Indians won 6–4.

272 **Great Expectations:** Thinking they had found the cure for their pitching woes, the Tribe brass promoted rookie Steve Dunning (1970–1973) to the majors directly out of Stanford University. Dunning won his first major league game on June 14, 1970, and pitched a one-hitter against the Washington Senators on April 18, 1971. That was about it for the good-looking right-hander. Steve was traded to the Texas Rangers in 1973 and was out of baseball by 1978.

273   **Indians Record:** The Tribe's all-time burglar in the base-stealing department is center fielder Kenny Lofton (1992–1996). Kenny stole 325 bases in his Indians career. He also holds the team record for bases snatched in a season, 75 in 1996.

274   **Tribe Trivia:** Only ten pitchers in American League history have ever struck out four batters in an inning (one batter reaching base on a dropped third strike). Believe it or not, four of these pitchers were Indians: Guy Morton (1916), Lee Stange (1964), Mike Paxton (1978), and Paul Shuey (1994).

275   **The angry reaction of Tribe fans** to club president Peter Bavasi's plan to permanently close the outfield bleachers in 1985. The bleachers were a familiar spot to many sunbathing fans, and Bavasi, an out-of-towner, soon got the message and compromised. He kept the bleachers open for day games

276 **Nicknames:** Walt "No Neck" Williams, OF, 1973. One look at a newspaper photo or a baseball card will quickly explain his nickname.

277 **The "Fog Game."** On May 27, 1986, the Indians and the Red Sox were "fogged-out" at Municipal Stadium. In the bottom of the sixth inning, the game was called due to fog, and Boston won 2–0. Actually, the game had been delayed twice before it was called. Indians' coach Bobby Bonds "tested" the visibility of the ball by hitting fly balls to outfielders each time before the game was resumed. Red Sox pitcher Dennis "Oil Can" Boyd complained that the stadium had been built too close to the ocean.

278 **Indians Luck:** While working as a scout for the Indians in 1948, Hugh Alexander was interested in scouting a young Oklahoma high school ballplayer. When talking to the boy's school principal, Alexander discovered that the boy had a bone disease in one of his legs, so he didn't make a date to see him play. That player's name? Mickey Mantle.

279 **Cleveland All-Star Games:** Cleveland played host to the All-Star Game for a record fifth time on July 8, 1997. Proudly displaying Jacobs Field to major league baseball's elite, the hometown crowd of 44,916 could not have been treated to a more dramatic midsummer classic. In the seventh inning, with the American and National Leagues tied at 1–1, Indians catcher Sandy Alomar homered to the left field bleachers with a runner on base to send the American League ahead to stay, 3–1. Alomar was named the game's MVP, the first time a player from the host team was honored as most valuable player.

Sandy steals the show

280 **Where's the Grease?** Over his entire major league career, including several years with the Indians, pitcher Gaylord Perry was the subject of many searches by plate umpires to find the grease with which he allegedly doctored the ball. Gaylord the Great played along with the drama as he touched his hat, jersey, glove, leg, and shoulder, giving fits to the umpires and opposing managers.

281 **The Replacement Indians of 1995.** With the major league players' strike of 1994 continuing into spring training of 1995, the Tribe was forced to field replacement teams comprised of minor leaguers and walk-on players. The replacement team played two exhibition games—one in Columbus, Ohio, against the Cincinnati Reds' replacements on April 1, 1995, and their final game against the New York Mets' replacements at Jacobs Field the following day. On April 2, 1995, regular major league players began returning as a tentative agreements were reached.

Replacements see end of line

282 **Good Trade:** In what amounted to a steal, the Indians sent outfielder/third baseman Paul Dade to the San Diego Padres for first baseman Mike Hargrove on June 14, 1979. Hargrove led the Indians with 85 runs batted-in in 1981 and batted over .300 three times in his six-year career with the Tribe. Dade faded from the major leagues after joining the Padres.

283 **The Cleveland Indians Old Timers Game of 1966.** Held at Cleveland Municipal Stadium on Sunday, June 12, 1966, this game was a chance to see baseball greats of the past up-close and personal. The roster included Bob Feller, Larry Doby, Joe Gordon, Mel Harder, Satchel Paige, Earl Averill, and even former owner Bill Veeck. The Indians greats signed autographs and played a short game, to the delight of fans.

284 **Great Expectations:** Neal Heaton looked like a promising fastball pitcher when he came to the Tribe in 1982. He started out with an 11–7 record in 1983 and a 12–15 record in 1984, and then slumped during the next two seasons. On June 20, 1986, he was traded to the Minnesota Twins for pitcher John Butcher.

Recollections . . .

Emil Bossard, Cleveland Indians groundskeeper (1935-1963).

"It's a game of inches. An inch is often the difference between a base hit and an out. We try to have the inches go our way."

285 **Family Affair:** Two Carreons had brief stints in Cleveland. Camilo Carreon caught 19 games for the Tribe in 1965 as a reserve catcher, and, 31 years later in 1996, son Mark played first base for Cleveland, batting .324 in 38 games.

286 **Second baseman Bobby Avila's sliding technique.** Avila would try to kick the ball out of the fielder's glove when sliding into a base. He was probably not well-liked by fellow second basemen. Avila played for the Tribe from 1949 to 1958.

287 **"Indian Fever," the Indians' 1978 theme song.** Everybody sing along: "Indian Fever, it's catchin' fire with everyone. Indian Fever, you can be part of the fun. It's the hits, the action, the double plays, it's how you feel when we win. Indian Fever, be a believer, with the Cleveland Indians." All the Tribe needed was on-field talent and the song would have sold millions.

288 **Indians Movies:** *Major League*, a 1988 Hollywood farce, portrayed a lowly Cleveland Indians team of misfits enjoying a miracle season and allowed Tribe fans the vicarious thrill of a fictional pennant race.

289 **One-Game Wonder:** On August 3, 1960, the Indians traded manager Joe Gordon to Detroit for Tiger manager Jimmy Dykes. Filling in for one day until Dykes arrived was Indians coach Jo Jo White, who skippered the Tribe to a 7–4 win over the Washington Senators.

290 **Nicknames:** "Silent George" Hendrick, OF, 1973–1976. A solid hitter, George refused to talk with the media from the day he entered major league baseball until his retirement in 1988.

291 **Indians Headdress:** In 1963, the Indians kept the navy-blue cap with the plain red wishbone "C" outlined in white but also added a red cap with a navy-blue wishbone "C" outlined in white, which became standard until 1970.

292 **Indians Books:** Want to learn what it was like during the Indians' hey-day of the 1948 season? This and other great accounts of the life and career of "boy-manager" Lou Boudreau are revealed in *Lou Boudreau—Covering All the Bases*, by Lou Boudreau with Russ Schneider (Sagamore Publishing, 1993).

293 **Indians Record:** Longest Game, Time. At Jacobs field on May 7, 1995, a 10–9 Tribe victory over the Minnesota Twins lasted 17-innings and went on for six hours and 36 minutes.

294 **Tribe Trivia:** Name pitching great Bob Feller's World Series victories for the Tribe. Stumped? "Rapid Robert," for all his accomplishments, never won a World Series game. In the 1948 Series, he lost the Opener 1–0, and the fifth game 11–5 to the Boston Braves. He never got the chance to pitch in the 1954 World Series, because the New York Giants swept the Indians in four straight games.

295 **Charles Lupica, the man atop the flagpole.** In 1949, Clevelander Charles Lupica was so convinced that the Tribe would repeat as American League champions that he bet friends he could sit atop a flagpole until the Indians won the pennant. On May 31, 1949, with the Indians in seventh place in the American League, Lupica climbed a 16-foot pole and occupied a covered platform until September 25, 1949, when the Indians were eliminated from the pennant race.

296 **Memorable Game:** In the first game of a doubleheader at Boston on July 14, 1946, Lou Boudreau hit four doubles and a home run. Ted Williams countered with three home runs of his own as the Red Sox beat the Tribe 11–10. In the second game, the famous "Boudreau Shift" was initiated to keep the slugging Ted Williams in check. Boudreau moved third baseman Ken Keltner behind second base, second baseman Jack Conway to short right field, himself to second base, and left fielder George Case into shallow left field.

297   **The price tag for the Cleveland Indians franchise** in 1940 as calculated by owner Alva Bradley—$1.8 million. In 1986, Richard and David Jacobs purchased the club from the F. J. O'Neill estate for $35.5 million and assumed $12 million in debts.

298   **Indians Hall of Famer:** An Indians backup catcher in 1947 and then the team's manager from 1951 to 1956, Al Lopez was later successful as a manager. After leading the Indians to the American League pennant and their best record ever in 1954 (111–43), he went on to manage the Chicago White Sox and lead them to the World Series in 1959. He was enshrined at Cooperstown in 1977.

299   **Good Trade:** On October 3, 1978, the Indians did some business with the Texas Rangers that reaped dividends down the road. They shipped relief pitcher Jim Kern and infielder Larvell Blanks to the Rangers for outfielder Bobby Bonds and pitcher Len Barker. Kern had some early success with Texas, but Blanks was a blank. Bonds hit very well for the Tribe in 1979, and Barker made baseball history on May 15, 1981, when he threw a perfect game against the Toronto Blue Jays.

Recollections . . .

Cary Seidman, Indians fan and teacher for the East Cleveland City Schools.

"On a warm summer night in 1966, I remember taking in a game at Municipal Stadium to see the Indians and the Minnesota Twins. Going into the last of the ninth, the Twins held a 3-2 lead. Indians second baseman Chico Salmon got a double with two outs. Billed as the Indians 'fastest man' by manager Birdie Tebbetts, Salmon represented the tying run. As Salmon reached second, the thunderstorm that had threatened for awhile broke out and delayed the game for over an hour. As fans gave up and went home, I stayed to watch what surely would be a tie and eventual win. When the game resumed, the Indians first baseman Fred Whitfield ripped the first pitch into right field for a single. From my seat in the upper deck, the scene was agonizingly clear. Twins outfielder Tony Oliva scooped up the ball and threw home. Our 'fastest man' legged it from second base but was a good 20 feet from home as the catcher held the ball, awaiting the ultimate tag. Just like that, game over."

300 **Indians Books:** *Now Pitching, Bob Feller*, by Bob Feller, with Bill Gilbert (Carol Publishing Group, 1990). Not only can Indians fans learn about Bob Feller's astounding career, but they can learn about Feller's views on baseball today—straight from the kid from Van Meter, Iowa!

301 **Spring training at Winter Haven, Florida.** Since 1993, the Tribe has called Winter Haven "home" for spring training. After 46 years in Tucson, Arizona, the Tribe was headed to a new complex in Homestead, Florida, until Hurricane Andrew devastated that area in 1992 and redirected the Tribe to Winter Haven's Chain-O-Lakes Park.

302 **Indians Hall of Famer:** Bill Veeck, owner of the Indians from 1946 to 1949, was one of baseball's most innovative promoters. After a fantastic world championship season in 1948, he sold the Tribe after the 1949 season. He subsequently owned the St. Louis Browns (1951–1953) and the Chicago White Sox (1959 and 1976–1980). He was enshrined at Cooperstown in 1991.

303 **Indians Luck:** Batting .304 and on pace to win the American League Rookie of the Year in 1963, Tribe center fielder Vic Davililo was hit by a pitch while facing left-hander Hank Aquirre of the Detroit Tigers on June 12, 1963. Davililo's right arm was broken, putting him out of commission for two months. Upon his return, the magic was gone, and Vic struggled against lefthanders for the rest of his career.

304 **Great Expectations:** Tribe brass thought they'd gamble on Bob Chance, a power-hitting first baseman/outfielder in 1963–1964. Nick-named "Baby Huey" because of his size and youthful face, Chance hit .281 with 16 home runs in 136 games for the Tribe and was traded to the Washington Senators in 1964.

305 **Mark McGwire's prodigious home run blast** on April 30, 1997. The Oakland slugger's blast hit the Budweiser sign (between the "e" and the "i") on the Jacobs Field scoreboard, 485 feet from home plate.

306 **The fine imposed on pitcher Sam McDowell,** determined by how far he threw a baseball into the stands after being ejected from a game during the 1969 season. Plate umpire Larry Barnett guessed that the ball fell 10 feet short of the top of the grandstand, about 205 rows up, making the fine $205. McDowell wrote a check for $216, claiming that he'd easily cleared the top of the grandstand—216 rows up!

307 **Memorable Game:** The last game of the 1995 regular season saw the Tribe wallop the Kansas City Royals 17–7. The Indians finished the season at 100–44, thirty games ahead of the second-place Royals—the largest margin of victory in major league baseball history. An exceptional feat, considering that the 1995 season was shortened to 144 games due to a players' strike, which ended in early April.

308 **Indians Headdress:** In 1978, the Tribe cap returned to a more conventional style, with a navy-blue cap, a red bill, and a red block "C" adorning the center of the hat.

Tribe All-Stars. Indians selected for the American League All-Star team four or more times include the following:

Bob Feller, P 1938, 1939, 1940, 1941, 1946, 1947, 1948, 1950

Lou Boudreau, SS, 1940, 1941, 1942, 1943, 1944, 1947, 1948

Larry Doby, OF, 1949, 1950, 1951, 1952, 1953, 1954, 1955

Ken Keltner, 3B, 1940, 1941, 1942, 1943, 1944, 1946, 1948

Bob Lemon, P 1948, 1949, 1950, 1951, 1952, 1953, 1954

Earl Averill, OF 1933, 1934, 1935, 1936, 1937, 1938

Sam McDowell, P, 1965, 1966, 1968, 1969, 1970, 1971

Jim Hegan, C, 1947, 1949, 1950, 1951, 1952

Sandy Alomar, C, 1990, 1991, 1992, 1996, 1997

Albert Belle, OF, 1993, 1994, 1995, 1996

Mel Harder, P, 1934, 1935, 1936, 1937

Al Rosen, 3B, 1952, 1953, 1954, 1955

310 **Clubhouse attendant Barney Godovin's good luck.** Godovin was hired by the Tribe in 1995 on a temporary basis. But when the Indians embarked on an 18-game winning streak after Barney was hired, manager Mike Hargrove made him a permanent fixture. "Good Luck Barney" started college in the fall of 1997.

311 **Nickname:** Dick "the Monster" Radatz. Acquired from the Boston Red Sox on June 2, 1966, to bolster a shaky bullpen, this premier relief pitcher turned out to be a bust for the Tribe. His imposing six-foot-four-inch height and mean fastball were ineffective, as Radatz appeared in just 42 games over two seasons.

312 **Broadcast partners Bob Neal and Jimmy Dudley.** While the two men shared the radio duties in 1957–1961 and 1965–1967, they simply did not like each other, and it often came through during their broadcasts. Dudley summed up their relationship: "Neal thought he should be number one and I *knew* I was number one."

Recollections . . .

Indians manager Mike Hargrove on the team's 1994 Opening Day 4-3 victory over the Seattle Mariners in their new home, Jacob's Field:

"I can't think of a better way to open this jewel of a ball park. It was scary for a while, but it ended perfectly."

313 **Chicken-wing pitchman Julian Tavarez.** During the 1996 season, the young reliever Tavarez appeared in a humorous television ad for the BW-3 restaurant chain. In the commercial, Julian—caught by an umpire with his hands sticky from eating chicken wings—smiled slyly and said, "well, maybe not for *me* . . . until *after* the game!"

314 **Ohio State football coach Woody Hayes,** acting like a fan instead of a coach, caught Tribe first baseman Vic Power's attention when he heckled him for acting like a "showboat." Power attempted to climb into the stands during the 1958 game at Municipal Stadium and give Woody a piece of his mind.

315 **Indians Books:** *Super Joe—The Life and Legend of Joe Charboneau,* by Joe Charboneau, with Burt Graeff and Terry Pluto (Stein and Day, 1981). Capitalizing on the frenzy surrounding Joe Charboneau's rookie year, this book described the life and lore surrounding Cleveland's most popular player since Rocky Colavito.

316 **Manager Pat Corrales' frequent trips to the pitcher's mound** during the 1984 season to order relief pitcher Ernie Camacho to throw a fast-ball, Ernie's best pitch. But Camacho insisted on throwing curves and off-speed pitches instead, prompting more angry marches to the mound.

317 **Indians Headdress:** Beginning in 1985, Chief Wahoo returned to grace the cap of Indians' players. It marked the first time since 1957 that the Chief appeared on the cap, but this time it was the caricature alone on a navy-blue cap with a red bill. A plain navy cap was introduced for road games in 1994.

318 **Opening Day:** The 1992 home opener at Municipal Stadium on April 11, 1992, provided Tribe fans with their own Boston marathon. Facing the Red Sox, the Indians battled for 19 innings, finally succumbing by a score of 7-5. The longest home opener on record, it lasted 6 ½ hours.

319   **Indians Hall of Famer:** Propping up a sagging Indians pitching staff from 1972 to 1975, Gaylord Perry was a bright spot in an otherwise bleak period for the Tribe. "Gaylord the Great" won the American League Cy Young Award for best pitcher in 1972 (and won it again in the National League in 1978), won 314 career games against 265 losses, struck out 3,534 batters, and ended up pitching for eight major league teams. He entered Cooperstown in 1991. Although he's enshrined as a member of the San Francisco Giants, Perry certainly had some of his "Hall of Fame" years with the Tribe.

320   **Jim Thome's back-to-back seasons of 30+ home runs.** Big Jim clubbed 38 homers in 1996 and 40 in the 1997 campaign. He became the first Indians left-handed hitter to hit 30 or more homers since first baseman Hal Trosky (1933–1941) did it in 1936 (42) and 1937 (32).

321   **Great Expectations:** What a difference three years make. The best Indians start to a season after 15 games was in 1966, when the Tribe went 14–1 under manager Birdie Tebbetts. Fortunes reversed in 1969, however, when they went 1–14 with manager Alvin Dark.

Recollections . . .

Indians coach Buddy Bell after Paul Sorrento's home run against the Toronto Blue Jays on June 4, 1995, in another 1995 come-from-behind victory. The Tribe won the game 9–8 after being down 7–0.

"I've never seen anything like this. I've never heard of anything like this, and I've never read anything like this. It's like you're in a dream and you never want to wake up."

322 **Memorable Game:** Facing the hated New York Yankees on September 23, 1997, the Tribe was looking to clinch a third straight central division championship. Hopes for victory were slim as the Tribe entered the sixth inning on the wrong side of a 9–2 score. Then came one of the more incredible comebacks in recent times. Hits by David Justice, Tony Fernandez, and Sandy Alomar sent fans and players alike into a wild frenzy as the Indians beat the Yanks, 10–9, in the bottom of the ninth.

323 **All-time Fan Favorites:** In 1969, fans were asked to select the greatest Indians team of all time. Does time change opinions? You decide.

1B Hal Trosky   OF "Shoeless" Joe Jackson

OF Charley Jamieson   3B Ken Keltner

2B Napoleon Lajoie   C Steve O'Neill

OF Tris Speaker   RHP Bob Feller

SS Lou Boudreau   LHP Vean Gregg

324

Tribe Top 10: Indians Pitching Wins

266 Bob Feller	157 Willis Hudlin
223 Mel Harder	147 George Uhle
207 Bob Lemon	142 Mike Garcia
172 Stan Coveleski	122 Jim Bagby, Sr.
164 Early Wynn	122 Sam McDowell
160 Addie Joss	

325

Memorable Game: On October 11, 1997, the Indians hosted the Baltimore Orioles at Jacobs Field in the third game of AL divisional series. Baltimore strikeout ace Mike Mussina recorded a major-league record 15 strikeouts in seven innings, but Indians pitcher Orel Hershiser kept his team in the ball game with seven shut-out innings of his own. With the game tied 1–1 in the bottom of the twelfth inning, Marquis Grissom sprinted home while Omar Vizquel's missed squeeze bunt got away from Orioles catcher Lenny Webster. The Indians won, 2–1.

326 **Memorable Game:** On October 15, 1997, in an appropriate finish to an incredible American League championship series, the Indians beat the Baltimore Orioles 1–0 at Orioles Park in Camden Yards. Again the Tribe faced Baltimore ace Mike Mussina, who struck out 10 in eight innings and compiled a league-championship record 25 Ks in two games. But Tribe pitcher Charles Nagy and the Indians bullpen pitched out of many jams and shut out the Orioles. The winning run came on second baseman Tony Fernandez's homer to right field in the eleventh. The Indians won the series four games to two; each victory was by a single run.

327 **Tough going:** The all-time toughest opponent for the Indians? You guessed it—the New York Yankees. The Tribe had a winning percentage of .446 against the Bronx Bombers through the end of the 1997 season.

1997 American League Champions

Indians roster for the World Series:

Manager: Mike Hargrove
Coaches: John Goryl, Luis Isaac, Charlie Manuel, Dave Nelson, Jeff Newman, Mark Wiley

#1 Tony Fernandez, 2B
#6 Bip Roberts, LF/2B
#7 Jeff Juden, P
#9 Matt Williams, 3B
#10 Pat Borders, C
#11 Jeff Branson, 2B
#12 Jeff Manto, 1B
#13 Omar Vizquel, SS
#15 Sandy Alomar, Jr., C
#17 Marquis Grissom, CF
#20 Kevin Seitzer, IF/DH

#22 Brian Giles, LF
#23 David Justice, LF/DH
#24 Manny Ramirez, RF
#25 Jim Thome, 1B
#27 Jaret Wright, P
#34 Brian Anderson, P
#37 Chad Ogea, P
#38 Eric Plunk, P
#41 Charles Nagy, P
#45 Paul Assenmacher, P
#48 Mike Jackson, P
#49 José Mesa, P
#51 Alvin Morman, P
#55 Orel Hershiser, P

Recollections . . .

Bill Needle, sportscaster for SportsChannel television.

"My earliest memories of the Indians are still the best. As a youngster, baseball was far more mysterious, less understood, and far more thrilling than today. My family lived in the Glenville area in the mid-1950s. My dad would drive to Municipal Stadium, and as we hit the shoreway at Eddy Road, I'd start to get excited. My excitement became unbearable as I caught a glimpse of the stadium's lights as we hit East 55th Street. There I was in the back of my dad's 1938 Chevrolet, holding my Fred Hatfield model Rawlings glove, waiting to get to the "ballgame." As I look back upon those times, I've wondered how many others felt their hearts beat faster as they approached the Stadium from either the east or west side and saw the lights aglow. I can still feel the anticipation as I think back to it."

329

All-Time Favorite Indians Team: *Favorite,* not necessarily *best.* Compile your favorite team with players from any year and compare:

Pos.	Tim's Favorite	Don's Favorite	Your Favorite
1B	Andre Thornton	Vic Power	
2B	Duane Kuiper	Bobby Avila	
3B	Max Alvis	Al Rosen	
SS	Omar Vizquel	Lou Boudreau	
OF	Rocky Colavito	Dale Mitchell	
OF	Kenny Lofton	Kenny Lofton	
OF	Leon Wagner	Larry Doby	
C	Sandy Alomar	Jim Hegan	
P	Luis Tiant	Bob Lemon	
P	Sam McDowell	Early Wynn	